Reviewed:

Theol 54 (1951) p. 276

THE BIBLE FROM WITHIN

THE
BIBLE FROM WITHIN

BY

A. G. HEBERT

of the Society of the Sacred Mission, Kelham
Doctor of Divinity

Geoffrey Cumberlege

OXFORD UNIVERSITY PRESS

LONDON   NEW YORK   TORONTO

1950

Oxford University Press, Amen House, London, E.C.4

GLASGOW NEW YORK TORONTO MELBOURNE WELLINGTON
BOMBAY CALCUTTA MADRAS CAPE TOWN

Geoffrey Cumberlege, Publisher to the University

Printed in Great Britain by
Butler & Tanner Ltd., Frome and London

Table of Contents

I. 'UNDERSTANDEST THOU WHAT THOU READEST?'   1
Introductory

II. 'BY THE WORD OF THE LORD WERE THE HEAVENS MADE'   12
The Creation: Genesis 1

III. 'AS IN ADAM ALL DIE . . .'   23
The Garden of Eden: Genesis 2–3

IV. 'ABRAHAM BELIEVED GOD'   34
The Stories in the Book of Genesis

V. 'THY WONDERS OF OLD TIME'   47
The Exodus and the subsequent history

VI. 'O ISRAEL, WHAT SHALL I DO UNTO THEE?'   63
Amos, Hosea, Isaiah, Deuteronomy

VII. 'CHASTENED AND NOT KILLED'   80
Jeremiah, Ezekiel, Second Isaiah

VIII. 'BEHOLD, THY KING COMETH UNTO THEE'   97
The Messianic prophecies

IX. 'THE LAW WAS OUR SCHOOLMASTER'   112
Haggai, Zechariah, Nehemiah, Ezra

X. 'LORD, WHAT LOVE HAVE I UNTO THY LAW'   125
Chronicles, Proverbs, Daniel, Psalm 119

XI. 'THE TIME IS FULFILLED'   141
The Gospel

XII. 'TO HIM BEAR ALL THE PROPHETS WITNESS'   171
The Christian use of the Old Testament

NOTE: *In the book-lists at the ends of chapters in this volume the British publisher and date of publication are given; the name of the U.S. publisher, if different from the British, is added at the end of the entry.*

CHAPTER I

'Understandest thou what thou readest?'

INTRODUCTORY

THE actual starting-point of this book was a question which was asked me in November, 1948, by a group of American clergy at the College of Preachers, Washington. They said: 'We need help for ourselves, and for our people, in understanding the particular texts which we read in the daily lessons in church. It is not enough to be told in a general way, that the Bible is the story of God's redemptive work and of His dealings with His people Israel, and that it is the Word of God. How can we hear the word of God spoken to us by this or that particular passage? Often it is difficult to make sense of it for ourselves; and it is more difficult for our people because in these days they mostly do not know their Bible. How do we begin in trying to help them make sense of it? This applies especially to the Old Testament. How are we, and they, to make profitable use of such and such a chapter of such and such a book?'

I was not prepared with an immediate answer to this question. It is not sufficient to speak of the 'devotional' use of the Bible, as if the use of Bible texts for the spiritual nourishment of the individual soul could be separated from the critical study of the Bible. Clergy and people are aware of the difficulties involved in the 'fundamentalist' view of the Bible, as being 'literally' true in every part; they know that the creation-story in Genesis, for instance, does not agree with the tale that is told by modern science, and that

I

the story of Adam and Eve is not literally true, and that there are many other difficulties which the fundamentalist view does not answer. But beyond this, there is the further difficulty that the Bible as a whole, and especially the Old Testament, seems to speak the language of a different world from that in which we live.

The ordinary ' critical ' books about the Bible give some help in making it real to us, and showing that the men and women of the Bible are real men and women. But these books about the Bible are largely occupied with technical questions : they discuss questions of archaeology, telling us of the recent discoveries at places like Lachish and Jericho ; or they give information about comparative religion, showing how the action of Jacob in pouring oil on the stone at Bethel in Genesis 28 is paralleled by the pouring of oil on stones in other ancient religions ; or they tell us how the Biblical account of creation can be compared with the Babylonian myths ; and they show how the books of the Bible are composed of different sources, and introduce us to J, E, D, and P.

If these things are true, as we are bound to think, they will certainly throw light on the meaning of the Bible ; and if the Bible is the word of God, these studies will certainly throw light on the word which God has spoken in it. But it is easy for the student of the Bible to find these studies very barren. They help us to see that the books of the Bible are human books, written by real men. But all this can easily be study *about* the Bible rather than *of* the Bible. It is rather as if the student of Shakespeare were to spend his time in investigating the sources from which Shakespeare drew the material for his plays, and the manner in which the plays were presented in an Elizabethan theatre. But we are not studying Shakespeare until we study the use he made of his materials, and appreciate for ourselves the greatness of his work. So it is with the Bible. All these questions which the 'critical' books raise are in truth only preliminary to the real study of the Bible, namely, the study of what it was that the Biblical writers actually said, the study of the Bible 'from within'.

This was the question which my friends were asking. Could they and their people be helped to get in touch with the actual word which such and such a writer was saying to the men of his own day and generation? That word, as he spoke it, was a living word, and it came to the men of that day as the word of the LORD, whether they were prepared to accept it as such, or not; and if we can grasp how it came as a living word to these men it will become a living word also to us.

But there is the difficulty that the world of the Bible was a very different world from that in which we live. This is, however, the case with all the literature of the past; with the poems of Homer or of Virgil or with Shakespeare's plays. We need some knowledge, however rudimentary, of the civilization in which a literature was produced, if we are to enter into it and profit by it. But this is not difficult, even for the ordinary reader; and it is readily possible for him to enter with imaginative sympathy into the books which have come down to us from the past.

So it is with the Bible. We believe that it is in a special sense the word of God. The story of Israel is a unique history, because Israel was the nation which the LORD God chose, that in it and through it He might carry out His saving Purpose for all mankind. Therefore, in reading the Bible we need to make contact with the men of the Bible as real men, of one flesh and blood with ourselves, and we need to see how in this history a real action of God took place. The Bible story is the story of the interaction of these two : God present and active in the events of history, and men responding with faith and love and obedience, or turning their backs and refusing to listen and obey.

GOD'S PURPOSE IN HISTORY

So then, if we take the Bible as a whole, we must learn to see in it the story of a continuous Purpose of God worked out in the history of Israel. This Purpose of God begins with the Call of Abraham, and with the Exodus of Israel from Egypt. It reaches its consummation in the coming of Jesus as the promised Messiah of Israel, and the admission of people of all nations to share in the knowledge of the true God which Israel had learnt, and become incorporated into the Israel of God as members of it side by side with Jewish Christians. Thus the Church to which we belong, is continuous with old Israel : it *is* Israel.

That is why the Bible is our book, the book of Israel, the book of the Church. The Jews of our Lord's day read it and used it, as explaining to them the Purpose of God by which Israel had come to be God's chosen nation, and different from all other nations. As such the Apostles of our Lord read it and used it, and they saw how the Purpose of God had reached its consummation in the Messiah. The Apostles' testimony is written down in the books of the New Testament which the Church later added to the canonical scriptures of the Old Testament. The complete Bible, consisting of Old and New Testament, tells us what the Church is. No one will understand the Bible if he reads it merely ' as literature ' : it can only be understood rightly when it is seen as the Book of the Church.

We have got into the way of thinking of the Church to which we belong as ' a denomination ', a society existing, by the side of other partly similar societies, for the practice of the Christian religion; for in our day Christendom has come to be divided into many denominations. But this way of thinking of 'a church' is unknown to the New Testament. There we do indeed read of 'the churches of Judaea' or 'the church of God which is at Corinth'; but these are only local names for the one Church existing in these various places. 'The Church' in the New Testament is 'the Israel of God', and the local communities are understood to be the local embodiments of the one Church, and that one Church to be continuous with the Israel of God which began in the days of Moses, but which was re-constituted by Jesus the Messiah, so that henceforth it might open its doors to men of all nations. Thus the conclusion of St. Paul's argument in Galatians, chapter 3, is that the Christians of Galatia, in spite of their heathen origin, are now in virtue of their baptism 'Abraham's seed' and heirs of the promises made to Abraham of old:

For as many of you as were baptized into Christ did put on Christ. There can be neither Jew nor Greek, there can be neither bond nor free, there can be no male and female: for ye are all One Man in Christ Jesus. And if ye are Christ's, then are ye Abraham's seed, heirs according to promise (Gal. 3. 27–9).

That which makes the Bible intelligible as a whole is the conception which runs through it of a Purpose of God in history. Perhaps this, more than anything else, can help the modern Christian reader to read and to love the Old Testament, if he can see that in the Bible history *something is happening*, something which it is necessary for him as a Christian to know, because it is essential to the understanding of his own Christian calling. In our schools much time is spent on the study of our national history, often out of all proportion to the study of the history of Europe and of civilization in general; this is justifiable because it is important that those who are to be citizens of their country should have a due sense of their national inheritance. So for us Christians the story of Old Israel is the story of our own past history and our own inheritance. The Church to which we belong has had a history, not merely of the nineteen hundred years since the time of our Lord, but of a period nearly twice as long, since the days of Abraham and Moses.

This conception of a Purpose of God in history is fundamental to the Bible. Again and again, as we read the Old Testament, we find Moses, or Joshua, or Samuel, represented as calling on the people to remember the works of the LORD God in their past history, and psalms such as 78, 105, 106, going over the history of the past in a spirit of thanksgiving and of penitence. The books from Genesis to Kings are in the form of a continuous history; another version of it comes in Chronicles and is continued in Ezra and Nehemiah. The prophets in their turn not only look back on the story of Israel's sinful past, but in the great Messianic prophecies look forward to a future divine action in which the great Purpose of God will reach its completion. The New Testament contains the announcement that 'the time [foretold by the prophets] is fulfilled, and the Kingdom of God [to which they looked forward] is at hand'; men must therefore 'repent, and believe the Gospel' (Mark 1. 15). For this is the Gospel; it is the Good Tidings that the Day of the LORD has now arrived, and the Purpose of God, to which the whole Old Testament looked forward, now reaches its consummation with the coming of the promised Messiah. This Gospel is declared to be for all nations; this is the theme, above all, of the Epistle to the Ephesians, which works out in detail how the reconciliation of man with God, and the remedy for sin which Christ has brought, leads to the calling in of people of all nations to share in that which had hitherto been the privilege of the one chosen nation. So it is that we, Christians of all nations, have entered on the inheritance of Israel; and the Bible, consisting of the Old and New Testaments, is the book which tells us what we are.

THE PLAN OF THIS BOOK

Our question was: How can the modern reader be helped to understand the books in detail, and make sense of such and such a chapter of such and such a book? We shall attempt to give some answer in the pages which follow. Plainly it will not be possible to deal with all the chapters of all the books; but it will be something if light can be thrown on some chapters of some books, and those the most important. We shall divide the history into periods, and try to see the books as belonging to those periods; and we must look, in the first place, not merely to the period which is described, but to the period in which the author was writing. For it stands to reason that he was writing in the first place for the men of his own day and generation; and if we are to understand what he was saying, we must learn to see what he was saying *to them*.

So, for instance, if the scholars tell us that some of the stories about Abraham were written, or orally narrated, about the time of Elijah, then we must try to imagine them as told to the people of that time, and see what it was that was being said to them; we should not, with the fundamentalist, take the story as an exact record of what happened to Abraham, nor, with the scholar who is interested in the ancient history of the Middle East, discuss primarily what fragments of historical truth may be extracted from the legends. Three hundred years later the Israelites were in exile; 'Lamentations' was written in a wholly different situation. Quite different again was the situation after the Return, when the 119th Psalm was written. In chapters IV to X we shall present a series of studies of some of the chief books in relation to the periods to which they belong.

It seems necessary, however, to begin by breaking into this scheme, and giving in chapters II and III studies of the creation-story and that of Adam and Eve, because those who arranged the Bible have chosen to begin with these, as providing a theological introduction to all that is to follow. We too need this theological introduction for ourselves. We shall therefore follow this order, even though here also, as we shall see, the historical situation in which the creation-story was written appears to be important to the understanding of it.

In chapter IV we continue with the Book of Genesis, and deal chiefly with the stories of Abraham, Jacob, and Joseph. Since, however, these were written during the period of the Monarchy, it is necessary first to take a glance at the series of books which tell of the story of Israel in Canaan. These books, of Joshua, Judges, Samuel, and Kings, are for the ordinary reader the simplest part of the Old Testament, as they present a continuous historical narrative; and this provides the framework within which the writers of the Genesis-stories lived.

In chapter V we go on to the Book of the Exodus. Here we shall be chiefly concerned with God's action in history, of which the Exodus of Israel from Egypt is a cardinal point. But the Bible narrative, both of the Exodus and of the subsequent history, is very different in style and character from our ordinary history-books, and we must inquire what is the point of view from which this history is told.

In chapter VI we come to an entirely different type of writing, the work of the great prophets, chiefly Amos,

Hosea, and Isaiah. They pronounce God's judgement on the national sin; and their books, with Revelation, chapter 18, remain the classical expression of His judgement on the sin of nations. In connexion with these, we take a look also at the Book of Deuteronomy, written largely under their influence, and containing a positive statement of the vocation of Israel to be God's People.

In chapter VII we continue with the history. The prophecies of doom were fulfilled in the catastrophe of the Fall of Jerusalem and the Exile. The whole national life was plucked up by the roots: how was it that Israel survived at all? It was indeed a marvel that it did survive; Israel died as a nation, and yet did not perish, but passed through a passion to a resurrection. Here the primary texts are some important passages from Jeremiah, Ezekiel, and the Second Isaiah.

Chapter VIII deals with the Messianic Hope; what had these prophets to say about God's future Purpose for His People? The First Isaiah had looked forward to a King of David's line. The prophets of the Exile foresaw a future time when the God who had delivered them at the Exodus from oppression in Egypt would work a new and greater deliverance, and would make them truly fit to be called His People, and would extend to all the nations the knowledge of Himself which Israel had gained.

In chapter IX we continue with the history. The difficulty is now that the Old Testament gives no further continuous narrative; yet this was a very important period in the history of the People of God. Ezra's Reform was the beginning of post-exilic Judaism.

Chapter X is concerned with the period after Ezra, showing four different aspects: the worship of the restored Temple, illustrated in the strong liturgical interest of the Book of

Chronicles; the Wisdom-literature, which made an approach to the Greek world; the attempt of the Greek world to destroy Israel in the Maccabean persecution, illustrated from the Book of Daniel; and the deepening, during this period, of the personal life of devotion, illustrated from Psalm 119.

Chapter XI brings us to the fulfilment of the whole Old Testament in Jesus Christ; in Him the divine Purpose reaches its consummation. Here the meaning of the Christian Redemption is studied under the same five headings under which the Messianic Hope was summarized in chapter VIII. What is meant by the Kingship of Christ, by Grace, by the Gift of the Holy Spirit, by the fulfilment of worship and sacrifice in the Church, and what is involved in the coming-in of the Gentiles to share in the inheritance of Israel?

Chapter XII is occupied with a look back at the Old Testament from the point of view of the New; for when the Old Testament has been fulfilled in Christ, it shines out with new meanings. The Law passes away but its permanent principles remain. The Old Testament (which speaks always in pictorial language) is full of types and anticipations of Christ and His cross; its broken lights find their completion in Him who is the Light of the World. The whole Bible, consisting of Old and New Testaments, is the Book of the Church.

NOTE ON THE DIVINE NAME

Every writer of a book on the Old Testament has the problem of how to write the Name of the God of Israel. In Hebrew it consists of four consonants, JHVH, and was probably pronounced *Yahweh*. In the later Biblical period the Jews, out of reverence, did not pronounce the sacred Name, but spoke instead the word *'Adonai*, 'lord', or 'my Lord'. In the old Hebrew script the consonants only were written; and when the vowels were added, they were written under or over the letters. Thus in a Hebrew Bible the consonants JHVH have the vowels of *'Adonai*; hence the hybrid word JEHOVAH. In the Greek Bible the sacred Name is translated *Kyrios*, Lord. In the English Bible JHVH regularly appears as 'the LORD', while 'Lord' represents *'Adonai*.

In books of scholarship 'Yahweh' is regularly used. In this book, 'the LORD' will be used for the most part. But often it is desirable to use 'Yahweh', especially where the context makes it necessary to emphasize that He who is the Maker of heaven and earth was also the tribal God of Israel.

A list of some books to which some sort of introduction is given

Genesis 1 (creation)	pp. 12–22	Proverbs	pp. 127–9
,, 2 (Adam and Eve)	23–9	Isaiah	68–74
,, 6–8 (the Flood)	73–4	Isaiah 40–55	102
,, 12–end	38–46	,, the Servant-poems	90–6
Exodus	47–56	Jeremiah	82–4
Deuteronomy	74–9	Ezekiel	82–6
Judges–Kings	34–8	Daniel	134–7
Chronicles	125–7	Hosea	66–8
Ezra and Nehemiah	112–16	Amos	64–6
Job	127	Jonah	121–2
Psalms	88, 183	Haggai and Zechariah	113

More detailed references are given in the index.

Some general books on the Bible :

C. F. Evans, *The Bible*. S.P.C.K., 1949.

C. H. Dodd, *The Bible To-day*. Cambridge University Press, 1947.

H. L. Goudge, *The Church and the Bible*. Longmans, 1930.

J. W. C. Wand, Bishop of London, *The Authority of the Scriptures*. Mowbray, 1949. (Morehouse.)

A. G. Hebert, *Scripture and the Faith*. Bles, 1947.

A. Richardson, *Preface to Bible Study*. S.C.M., 1944. (Macmillan.)

T. W. Manson (ed.), *A Companion to the Bible*. T. & T. Clark, 1939. (Scribner.)

W. K. Lowther Clarke, *A Little Dictionary of Bible Phrases*. S.P.C.K., 1938. (Macmillan.)

CHAPTER II

' *By the word of the* LORD *were the heavens made* '

THE CREATION: GENESIS 1 and 2. 1–4

THOSE who edited the Book of Genesis and put together the five 'books of Moses' (the Pentateuch), began not with the beginning of the tribal history, but with the beginning of the Universe. 'In the beginning God created the heaven and the earth.' They did this because they believed that the history of their own nation which they were going to relate was of importance for all nations and all men everywhere.

Later in this book we shall consider the period to which scholars assign this creation-story: it was written in the time of the Exile, when the Israelites were living in the midst of the great Babylonian civilization, amidst the worship of the Babylonian gods Bel and Nebo, themselves believing that Yahweh the God of Israel was the true and only God; when also their prophets were declaring that the time would come when the knowledge of Him which Israel possessed would be shared by all nations;

> Look unto me and be ye saved,
> All the ends of the earth,
> For I am God,
> And there is none else.
> By myself have I sworn—
>> The word is gone forth from my mouth in righteousness
>> And shall not return
> That unto me every knee shall bow
> Every tongue shall swear (Isa. 45. 22–3).

These words are taken from the great prophet of the Exile whom we call the Second Isaiah, and thus date from much the same period as the first chapter of Genesis.

Scholars have pointed out how a number of phrases of Genesis 1 correspond to the Babylonian accounts of the creation which have been preserved on the clay tablets of the period : such for instance as ' the deep ' and ' the firmament '. The deep, Heb. *Tehom*, is the Babylonian *Tiamtu* or *Tiamat*, of which the Babylonian creation-story says :

> He cleft her [*Tiamat*] like a fish . . . in two halves,
> From the one half he made and covered the heaven,
> He drew a barrier, placed sentinels,
> Commanded not to let its waters through.

It is indeed probable that the Babylonian creation-story was known to the Israelites long before the Exile. But if Genesis 1 was written during the Exile, it was written in the country to which the Babylonian creation-story belonged, and would at once challenge comparison with it. The outstanding point is that the Babylonian story is polytheistic ; there are many gods, of the heaven above and of the depth beneath. In Genesis 1 God is one alone.

We can therefore rightly compare this first chapter of Genesis with the passages in Second Isaiah where the gods of the heathen are ridiculed as no-gods, and it is proclaimed with the greatest vigour that Yahweh alone is the living and true God : He who has revealed Himself to Israel His chosen people, whom of old He brought out of Egypt, and who controls the course of history. By His prophets He had announced the judgement that was to fall on Israel His People, and this word had come true when Jerusalem was destroyed. But the gods of the heathen are unreal ; they can do nothing and can originate nothing :

Let them bring them forth, and declare unto us what shall happen : declare ye the former things, what they be, that we may consider them, and know the latter end of them ; or show us things for to come. Declare the things that are to come after, that we may know that ye are gods ; yea, do good, or do evil, that we may be dismayed and behold it together. Behold, ye are of nothing, and your work of nought ; an abomination is he that chooseth you (Isa. 41. 22–4).

In 44. 9–20 there is a highly sarcastic description of a man making an image of a god, using the waste parts of the wood to make a fire and cook his dinner, and fashioning the rest into a god, to which he bows down in worship. In 46. 1–2, at the predicted fall of Babylon, Bel and Nebo are pictured as loaded up on the back of weary animals, and carried off. But as for Yahweh,

> Even to old age I am He,
> And even to hoar hairs will I carry you ;
> I have made, and I will bear ;
> Yea, I will carry, and will deliver.
> To whom will ye liken me, and make me equal,
> And compare me, that we may be like ? (Isa. 46. 4–5).

And He is the creator :

> Thus saith the LORD, that created the heavens,
> He is God, that formed the earth and made it :
>   He established it, he created it not a waste,
>   He formed it to be inhabited.
> I am the LORD, and there is none else (Isa. 45. 18 ; cf. 48. 12–13).

These words of Second Isaiah throw real light on what the writer of Genesis intended to say. By the side of his majestic narrative the Babylonian creation-poems would look very mean and unworthy. He wrote it as an act of praise to the LORD, whose glory is revealed in the order and beauty of His created world. Within that creation is man, different from the animals by the fact that he is made in God's own image, capable of beholding God's glory revealed in His works, and commanded to keep Sabbath, week by week, after the pattern of Him who 'rested on the seventh day' and 'blessed the seventh day and hallowed it' (Gen. 2. 2–3).

THE DOCTRINE OF THE CREATION

What, then, is the importance of the creation-story for us ? First, those who insist that because the Bible is the word of God, therefore the creation-story must be 'literally' true from the standpoint of astronomy, geology, and biology, invite the immediate retort that the creation-story is not true from the standpoint of astronomy, geology, and biology, therefore the Bible is not the word of God. Further, in taking the story as in this sense 'literally' and absolutely true, they are failing to seek to learn what it was that the writer intended to say to his own day and generation, and thereby failing to learn what he really has to say to us. Yet again, to take the story as true in that absolute sense, is to deny the truth which the writer proclaims, that God made man in His own image. They are taking the story as foreclosing the investigations of the scientist, by providing him beforehand with the answers which he must reach to scientific questions. But if God really did make man 'in His own image', He surely intended man to use the powers which He had given him. We are bound, therefore, to refuse the fundamentalist's answer for theological reasons, and not because 'science has proved the Bible to be wrong'.

Then : if the creation-story is taken as theologically true, are we to value it as providing the material for the doctrine of the creation of the world by God, which shall form the first chapter of a scheme of systematic theology ? Do we say :

' Now we are in a position to state the idea of God in relation to His created world, and we will go on from this to build up a structure of ordered knowledge about God and the universe and man ? ' It is safe to say that such an idea is far from the mind of the Biblical writers. The Bible is dogmatic from end to end, but it never gives us a systematic theology. The Hebrew writers are not concerned to see how God fits into our scheme of things : they are greatly concerned to see how we fit into His.

They are not chiefly concerned to provide accurate statements of our ideas about God. They are concerned to present Him to our minds as the underlying reality and ground of all existence. ' Thou hast laid the foundation of the earth ', they say, ' and it abideth ' : the sun and moon and stars; the habitable earth; the plants and animals; man made in His image, male and female; the order and structure of human life—all this depends on God, irrespective of whether men do or do not believe in Him and know Him. ' And God saw all that He had made, and behold it was very good.'

The truth of the real God who has made man in His own image is asserted in the Bible as against the false belief of men in the gods whom they have made in their own image; personifications of natural forces, or personifications of the genius of some tribe or nation. We shall see in later chapters how the Israelites in Canaan were led away to worship the Canaanite Baals who made the corn grow, gods whose favour it was necessary to secure in order to get a good harvest; and how the gods of Moab and Syria and the surrounding tribes were symbols of the genius of the tribe, so that if the tribe was overwhelmed in war, it was because its god had been defeated and overpowered. But Israel believed in a God who had chosen it to be His people, and could and did chastise and punish it when it sinned against Him ; and a God who did indeed make the corn grow, for He was the Giver of all, but whose favour was not to be bought by sacrifices and gifts.

We make a great mistake if we think that we whose civilization has developed so far above the level of those primitive days, need not trouble much about the doctrine of God the creator, as if this were an elementary truth which we can now take for granted. The outward setting has changed, and the names have changed : the fundamental issue remains much the same. Multitudes of people to-day worship false gods. There is the god of Luck : witness the betting and gambling and lotteries and football pools. There is the god or goddess of Lust, drawing a crowd of devotees. There is Mammon, the passion for money-making for the sake of the comforts which it buys, the power over other people's lives which it gives, or the pride of victory in the competition of wits. There is Nationalism, which indeed has altered little from what it was in those old days, except in the vast resources which it has at its disposal both as regards material means of destruction and the power of propaganda to carry the minds of men away in its lust of power.

Yet again, the truth of God the creator is denied in the notion that the universe is controlled by forces of nature which are morally neutral, and provide an arena on which the conflict of good and evil in men's lives goes on. That is why it seems to most people absurd to pray for rain ; for is not the weather controlled entirely by atmospheric forces, which may indeed be too complex for the meteorological experts to predict, but which at any rate lie outside the control of 'God'? Those who believe that God exists are often unconscious Deists, thinking that God created the world in its far-away beginning, but not thinking of Him as present and active in it, sending the springs into the rivers which run among the hills, bringing forth grass for the cattle, and herb for the service of man, that He may bring food out of the earth, and wine and oil and bread (Ps. 104. 10–15), and not thinking that all that happens happens by His never-failing providence ordering all things in heaven and earth.

MAN IN GOD'S IMAGE

With the truth of God as creator goes the doctrine of man, who, as Gen. 1. 26 says, is 'made in God's image'. Man is not able to create universes; but he is endowed with a spark of creative power. He can think and speculate what the plan of God's universe may be; and using the materials which lie to his hand in his created existence, he can shape and fashion these to express creative ideas. Artistic self-expression, by painting, sculpture, architecture, music, poetry, by the style in which he furnishes a home and orders his life, is the law of his nature. He is within the natural order, by the fact that he has a body; but he is not a mere cog in a machine, but is able to stand outside it, survey it, pronounce judgements on it.

He has a sense of truth : that there is a truth which can be reached by disinterested and unprejudiced research, in which the personal desires of the investigator and all wishful thinking are as far as possible eliminated, and that this apprehension of truth, though always limited and imperfect, is nevertheless real. Such is the way of scientific research.

Second, he has a sense of a right and wrong which are independent of the desires and ambitions of men. The fact that a practice or habit exists is no proof that it is good ; opium-smoking is an instance. Might is no criterion of

Right. There is a good worth living for, and therefore also worth dying for.

Third, he is subject to Law, not merely to the 'positive law' of state legislation, but to the higher 'natural law' by which the law of the state is to be judged. In civilized nations conscientious objectors are allowed the freedom that they demand, even by judges who regard them as self-opiniated and stupid people. Again, in civilized nations it is a fundamental principle that the Judiciary must be separate from the Executive: in other words, that those who preside in the law-courts shall not be responsible to the Government in power. The State must not be judge in its own case.

Fourth, he believes that there is a common humanity which possesses rights. The true principle of Democracy is that the citizens are not mere members of a hive, but possess a certain authority in relation to the affairs of the hive. They are men, and have a right to sit in judgement on the actions of the State, and criticize the laws which they obey.

These are the permanent principles on which our civilization has stood. But they depend on a doctrine of the nature of man which is ultimately a theological doctrine; for this doctrine of man asserts that he is something more than an animal, something more than a bundle of psychological impulses, something more than a mere unit in a social organism. He belongs to the created order, he is moulded by heredity and environment; but he is also a person. The fact that he is a person means that he belongs also to an eternal order, has a sense of truth and a sense of right, and can believe in God. When therefore the creation-story in Gen. 1 says that man is made in God's image, it is proclaiming man's freedom and man's character as a responsible person.

Recent history has made it clear that when belief in God

is denied, every one of the four points that we have stated is denied too. Men are treated as subjects for ' conditioning ' or for propaganda ; right comes to be identified with the claims of the totalitarian state ; the State insists in being judge in its own cause ; and the rights of common humanity are set at naught. It is further true that these fundamental principles which the totalitarian states deny outright are in peril of being continuously whittled away in the so-called Democracies.

In sharp contrast with this stands not only the key-phrase of Gen. 1. 26, but also its further explication in the doctrine of the Trinity, which, translated into terms of the doctrine of Man, asserts that man is the sort of creature that can call on God as Father and adore Him as creator ; whose nature the Son of God could take on Himself when He was made man, and for whose salvation He could die : and in whose heart God the Holy Ghost can come and dwell, leading him into all truth.

CREATION AND REDEMPTION

In the New Testament the Redemption is treated as the renewal and restoration of that which God created in the beginning. It is not that by the redemptive work of Jesus Christ man is rescued from entanglement with the body and with the created order generally—as if man were thereby raised from preoccupation with the ordinary concerns of life into some region of Higher Thought, and initiated into some theosophical secret lore. It is that the Son of Man in His Incarnation became true man, living in a home, working in a carpenter's shop, and facing death as we all must :

Since then the children [i.e. men] are sharers in flesh and blood, he also himself in like manner partook of the same ; that through death he might bring to nought him that had the power of death, that is, the devil, and might deliver all them who through fear of death were all their lifetime subject to bondage (Heb. 2. 14–15);

and sharing our suffering and our temptation:

For we have not a High Priest that cannot be touched with the feeling of our infirmities, but one that hath been in all points tempted like as we are, yet without sin (4. 15).

He suffered in the Garden of Gethsemane:

Who in the days of his flesh, having offered up prayers and supplications with strong crying and tears unto him that was able to save him from death, and having been heard for his godly fear, though he was a Son, yet learned obedience by the things which he suffered; and having been made perfect, he became unto all them that obey him the author of eternal salvation (5. 7–9).

It is our human life, as it is lived under ordinary human conditions, that is redeemed to God and sanctified. That which God created is redeemed.

It is for this reason that the prologue of St. John's Gospel, which tells how the Word was made flesh, that all that believe on His name might become sons of God, begins with the same words as Gen. 1. 1: ' In the beginning . . .' St. Paul too in several places speaks of the Redemption as a second creation, as when he echoes the phrases of Isa. 65. 17, ' Behold I create new heavens and a new earth, and the former things shall not be remembered, nor come into mind ', in the words of 2 Cor. 5. 17: ' Wherefore if any man is in Christ, he is a new creature: the old things are passed away; behold they are become new ', through the work of God who ' in Christ was reconciling the world to Himself' (5. 19). ' A new heaven and a new earth ' are spoken of in Rev. 21. 1, with reference primarily to the Future World which begins with the Second Advent, in the life beyond death. But the New Testament teaching is that this 'new creation' begins with the First Advent, when the Son of God came in the flesh as true man, to restore and renew our human nature ; that same human nature which He created in the beginning.

F. E. Coggin, *The First Story of Genesis as Literature*.   Heffer, Cambridge, 1932.

S. R. Driver, *Genesis* (Westminster Commentaries), 1904.

On the doctrine of Man :

V. A. Demant, *The Religious Prospect*.   Muller, 1939.

A. G. Hebert, *The Christian Doctrine of Man*.   Industrial Christian Fellowship, 1 Broadway, London, S.W.1.   (A single lecture.)

CHAPTER III

' *As in Adam all die . . .* '

THE GARDEN OF EDEN: GENESIS 2-3

THE story of Adam and Eve is by a different writer, and it was written before the Exile; it is clear that when we come to Gen. 2. 4 we pass to a quite different style. But those who compiled our book of Genesis placed this account of Man's life in the world, first as God meant it to be, then as it actually is, next after the great poem of the creation. The writer is telling us, in the form of a tale, about Man's life in general; this is clear from the fact that the Hebrew word *'adam* means simply ' man ', and so is not a proper name. The story of Adam and Eve is a common subject for mockery; but the mockery is out of place, for the writer has exceedingly profound things to say to us about ourselves, as we shall seek to show. He has chosen the form of a Tale as the most suitable means for expressing his meaning; and so indeed it is.

Was there a Fall of Man? Was there a first sin? Probably the dogmatic theologian will wish to say that there was. But he is compelled to add that this story in Gen. 2 and 3 cannot possibly be a historical record of the event; no historian could assert that it has any claim to be an authentic memory, handed down in a historical tradition. It comes to us as a Tale, embodying some vital truths about human nature.

MAN'S ORIGINAL AND PROPER CONDITION

First the writer shows us Man's right and proper condition, as God intended him to be. Let us begin with

2. 15 : 'The Lord God took the Man, and put him into the Garden of Eden, to dress it and to keep it.' We are in the world 'to dress it and to keep it' : to till the soil, build houses, make roads and harbours, get the coal, build up a civilization. 2. 16 : 'of every tree in the garden thou mayest freely eat' : we have a free hand, we are to use our discretion, and do as we will. But (2. 18) there are things that we must not do : 'the tree of the knowledge of good and evil, thou shalt not eat of it, for in the day that thou eatest thereof thou shalt surely die'. We must say more of the penalty of death later, and of the meaning of 'know-ledge of good and evil'; indeed, on the correct under-standing of these two points the whole interpretation of the story of the Fall depends. But, leaving these for the moment, we have this clear point : that we are free to do as we will in God's world, but we are subject to His law. While Man so lives, obedient to His will, and receiving everything from Him as His gift, and giving Him thanks for everything, all is well.

2. 18 : 'It is not good that the Man should be alone'; he needs a help suited to him, a companion for life. Such companionship the animals cannot provide. 2. 19, 20 : the animals are with the Man in the world, and the LORD God shows them to him, and he gives them names. This we have done. But, 2. 20, the animals cannot provide the companionship he needs; 'for Man there was not found a help meet for him'. Then 2. 21–2 : the LORD God brings the Woman to the Man. When he sees the Woman, the Man bursts into the first primal love-song, the type of all his love-songs ever since : ' *This* is now bone of my bones, and flesh of my flesh : *this* shall be called Woman ['*Ishshah*], for *this* was taken out of Man ['*Ish*].' The Man has the 'help meet for him'; he recognizes the Woman as the

missing half of himself; he was made for her, and she for him. 2. 24: the writer digresses to point out that here is the primal ordinance of Marriage.

We have seen God's ordinance for Man, the pattern of human life, as it was meant to be, lived in God's world and in dependence upon Him. Now we come to Man's actual condition, and hear the story of the Fall.

THE FALL OF MAN AND HIS PRESENT CONDITION

3. 1: 'The Serpent' is not explained. No doubt we shall identify it with Satan; but this is not done in the Tale, where nothing is said of the origin of the power of evil to beguile and deceive, and the fact of beguilement and temptation is just accepted. 3. 2–3: the Serpent asks the Woman about the condition of their life, and she tells it. Then it says, 3. 4, 'Ye shall not surely die, for God doth know that in the day ye eat thereof, your eyes shall be opened, and ye shall be as God, knowing good and evil.' What does this mean?

The Serpent tells them that they will not die, if they break God's law; and seemingly this is quite true, for according to the course of events in the Tale, they do not immediately die, but go on living for a long time, and sons are born to them. But assuredly the writer did not mean that the penalty of death was an idle threat, or a piece of bluff, on God's part. We had best look at the actual consequences of their act; they are as follows:

3. 7: they become aware that they are naked, and are ashamed of it. 3. 8: they run away from God; they 'hid themselves from the presence of the LORD among the trees of the garden'; and they had never done this before. 3. 12: when they are called to account for their action, the Man forgets all that he had said about the Woman being

25

' bone of his bone and flesh of his flesh ' ; he speaks of her as
' the Woman whom thou gavest to be with me,' another
individual with whom he must get along somehow. There
is indeed a change in him ; and we read as we go on how
(3. 16) to the Woman childbirth is to be hard and painful and
(3. 17) to the Man labour becomes drudgery. And then
(3. 23) the Man and the Woman have to be turned out of
the garden where they have lived in God's presence.

Does not this throw light on the meaning which the writer
intends to give to the penalty of death ? It has often been
assumed that ' death ' means the death of the body, and
those who have taken the story of the Fall as ' literally true '
have believed that man before the Fall was immortal ; this,
however, is impossible for us to take seriously, since we
know that Man has evolved from lower forms of life,
and death is universal in the animal creation. But the writer
cannot have meant this, since it is inconsistent with the course
of his own tale. The Serpent indeed so interprets the
penalty of death ; but the Serpent's mind is bounded by
its narrowly materialistic outlook. Actually in the story
that which happens to Man is something much worse than
bodily death. That which dies in him is his manhood. If
we look on further in the Bible we find this thought expressed
by St. Paul in Rom. 8. 6–7 : ' The mind of the flesh *is*
death,' for ' the mind of the flesh *is* enmity against God '.

But now, what is their sin ? Is it the mere transgression
of an arbitrary command, the doing of something not wrong
in itself, and only wrong because it has been forbidden ?
We might compare the rule forbidding the Jews to eat pork,
which is in itself good food. But if we have already seen
reason to think that this writer has very wise things to say,
we ought to suspect that the meaning of the prohibition
goes deeper than that. Let us inquire, then, into the mean-

ing of 'knowing good and evil'. Does it mean 'knowing the difference between right and wrong', by doing evil and so knowing what evil is? That is commonly assumed to be the meaning.

But quite apart from the phrase in 3. 4: 'Ye shall be as God, knowing good and evil,' which on this interpretation would imply that God must do wrong in order to know what it is, this assumption is not consistent with the meaning of 'knowing good and evil' in the other places where it occurs in the Old Testament. There the meaning is consistently the same. 'Knowledge of good and evil' is the attainment of *savoir faire*, sagacity, and capacity to deal with affairs, to which a child attains as it grows up. Infants are without it (Deut. 1. 39; Isa. 7. 15–16); an old man of eighty says in 2 Sam. 19. 35 that he is, as we should put it, 'in his second childhood'. In Gen. 24. 50 a similar phrase comes, with the meaning that the matter in hand has been settled by divine guidance, and cannot be argued on grounds of worldly prudence. Most clearly of all, when young King Solomon is asked by God in a dream what he will have (1 Kings 3. 9), he asks that he may have an understanding heart to judge the people, and 'discern between good and evil', and the gift is granted. What Solomon receives is not conscientiousness, but sagacity, prudence, astuteness; this is illustrated by his cleverness in dealing with the problem of the two women with one living baby (1 Kings 3. 16–28).

What then is the sin? To desire to be as God, knowing good and evil; to grow up to the stature of manhood in their own way, worshipping the self instead of God; to develop their intelligence and resourcefulness and capacity to deal with affairs, regardless of God. The Serpent had suggested (3. 5) that God was keeping something back from them: well then, let them take the course of their lives into

27   C

their own hands, and (instead of being content to receive from Him in dependence and thankfulness the development of their own powers) insist on grabbing at the good things of life, in order to possess them for themselves and grow up in their own way and not His.

Something like this is surely what the writer intends us to understand. And such is human life as we know it and as he knew it too. And when we have read a little further in the Book of Genesis we come to the words ' The earth was corrupt before God, and the earth was filled with violence . . . for all flesh had corrupted his way upon the earth' (6. 11–12). Such is the world as we know it, a dark and sinful world.

And yet God has not left Himself without witness, nor is Man totally depraved. As F. D. Maurice says : ' Brutal violence, men corrupting their ways upon the earth—this is just what we hear of everywhere. Scripture had nothing new to tell us about this. But it had a work of its own. It had to teach us how these facts are compatible with others, apparently quite at variance with them, which ordinary history and our own experience also make known to us. It had to show how this natural corruption could co-exist with a perpetual witness in man's conscience, with a continual strife in his will, against it. And it does this work. It shows us that man, yielding to his nature, resists the law which he was created to obey ; that man, given up to himself, yet has God's Spirit striving with him. It shows us how man in himself can have no good thing, and yet how much good he may have, because there is One Who is continually raising him out of himself, imparting to him that which in his own nature he has not' (F. D. Maurice, *Patriarchs and Lawgivers of the Old Testament*, p. 62).

But are we perhaps reading too much into this tale ? Are

28

we finding things in it which the writer did not intend? In a case such as this there are two opposite dangers. One is the tendency to despise in our hearts these writers who lived so long ago, in an age that was in some respects so barbaric; and this is a fault of which many modern books on the Old Testament have been guilty. Yet no one treats Homer in this way; and the author of the story of the Fall was a poet too, and one who deserves to be treated with the greatest respect. The opposite danger is that of reading back into his work conceptions which only became articulate and fully defined after much fuller reflection and, above all, after the experience which the Gospel of Christ has brought. It may well be that our exposition lies open in some measure to this charge. Yet assuredly it lies in the right direction; the writer clearly saw that the essence of Sin lies in a wrong relation to the personal God.

WHAT IS SIN?

Such a view of Sin is certainly characteristic of the Old Testament. It is often said, indeed, that the Old Testament is legalistic, providing us with commandments to keep, where the New Testament gives us principles to follow; that the Old Covenant was one of Law, and the New Covenant one of Grace. It is true indeed that the Judaism of the last three or four centuries before Christ did emphasize law-keeping very strongly; the Pharisees in our Lord's day did so. But that is not true of the Old Testament as a whole; the prophets and the psalmists speak throughout of the personal relation between God and His People, and think of Sin not as the mere breach of an imposed rule, but as unfaithfulness to the personal God.

If we would satisfy ourselves that this really is the general view of Sin in the Old Testament, it is easy to do so by a

simple experiment, which is rather like the sinking of a shaft
by a mining engineer in order to find whether there is coal
underground. Look up the words 'transgress' and 'transgression' as they occur in the Authorized Version, in *Young's
Analytical Concordance*, which not only gives the places where
the English word occurs, but divides it up according to the
several Hebrew or Greek words which it represents. This
is a rough test, but a reliable one; and what one finds is
this. There are four Hebrew words which are translated
'transgress'; *bagad*, *ma'al*, *'abar*, and *pasha'*. *Bagad* means
to 'deal treacherously' with God; the same Hebrew word
is used in Judges 9. 23, 'the men of Shechem dealt treacherously with Abimelech', in the course of the rather sordid
tale of his attempt to reign over them. The next word,
ma'al, means an act of wrongdoing, a trespass or transgression, as when in Neh. 13. 27 some Jews have transgressed
the prohibition against marrying foreign wives. The next
is *'abar*, which means 'to pass by', and in this connexion
to 'go the other way', as when I see someone in the distance
whom I do not wish to meet, and walk off in another direction; so the word is used in Prov. 4. 15, of the 'way of
wicked men', 'avoid it, pass not by it; turn from it and
pass on'. The fourth word translated 'transgress', *pasha'*,
means simply 'to rebel', and is used in 2 Kings 1. 1: 'Moab
rebelled against Israel after the death of Ahab.'

Here we have four words translated 'transgress', which
taken together throw a truly remarkable light on the meaning
of Sin. One of the four means 'breaking the rules', and it is
interesting to see that this word occurs most often in books
dating from the post-exilic period, which was the time of
Jewish legalism. The other three express in vivid pictorial
ways the meaning of sin against the personal God: to
'deal treacherously', to 'walk the other way', to 'rebel'.

ORIGINAL SIN

This brings us to the further question : What do we mean by Original Sin ? This is a large question, and to deal properly with the Biblical teaching about Sin a big book would be needed. But we are commenting on the tale in Gen. 3 ; and in spite of the fact that the tale necessarily speaks of an act of sin, we ought not to think of a white robe of personal innocence now defiled by an ugly stain. This is not admissible, because the name ' Adam ', meaning ' Man ', and the name ' Eve ', meaning ' Life ', show that the Man and the Woman are not being thought of as individuals in history. Their sin is the sin of Man ; and as the whole pattern of the story shows, that which is being described is the passing of Man from a right relation to God (dependence, thankfulness, obedience) to a wrong relation (independence, rebelliousness, alienation). Man chooses to live without God.

When we so view Man's condition, the metaphor of the stain on the white garment is seen at once to be seriously misleading. It is not that Man has now a stain on his moral character, so that he can no longer have a good opinion of himself and consider himself a meritorious and worthy person. It is that Man himself is wrong, aiming in the wrong direction ; and this is the idea denoted by the Greek word for sin, *hamartia*. Here we have the distinction between *hamartia*, Sin (with a capital S), and *hamartēmata*, sins : it is a distinction which the Latin language fails to reproduce, so that we still sing (incorrectly) ' O Lamb of God, that takest away the sins of the world,' when the Greek word in John 1. 29 is the word which means Sin.

Here we have the distinction of actual sin and Original Sin. Actual sin is *acts* committed by such and such a person

31

at such and such a time, by thought, word or deed ; Original Sin is the *state* of alienation from God which lies behind. It is a pity if we think of Original Sin legalistically, as if it were a sort of entail, or something which renders us 'prone' to commit actual sins. We do better if we take a lesson from Article IX, which explains Original Sin by referring to the *phronēma sarkos*, or 'mind of the flesh', of which St. Paul speaks in Rom. 8. 6–8 : 'The mind of the flesh is death, but the mind of the Spirit is life and peace ; because the mind of the flesh is enmity against God, for it is not subject to the law of God, neither indeed can it be ; and they that are "in the flesh" cannot please God.'

Here 'flesh' and 'Spirit' are opposed. 'Flesh' cannot in this passage mean 'our physical nature', for in that case the last clause would mean 'no one in this life can please God'; and St. Paul proceeds (8. 9) 'But ye are not "in the flesh" but in the Spirit, if so be that the Spirit of God dwelleth in you.' He defines the 'mind of the flesh' as 'enmity against God'. It is the attitude of self-centred-ness, self-love, the idolatry of the self in place of the worship of God ; and as St. Paul had known in his life as a Pharisee, it is entirely compatible with an earnest and self-denying religiousness. 'I thank Thee,' said the Pharisee, 'that I am not as other men are, or even as this Publican.' Someone has said that to-day there are Publicans who are found saying, 'I thank Thee that I am not as this Pharisee, for at least my sins are interesting sins.'

The escape from this enmity or alienation (which is Original Sin) cannot be effected by the Self, for then it would have cause to take pride in its own ingenuity in contriving its escape, and manipulating the proper psychological strings to bring about its own conversion. The one way of escape is that the means of escape should be provided by God

Himself, and be received by Man as a gift: and such is the Christian Gospel. 'Herein is love, not that we loved God, but that he loved us, and sent his Son . . .' (1 John 4. 10). To the soul, convicted of its own sin, and awakened to a response to the mighty love of God which has set it free, the only possible right attitude is humility, namely to see the Self in its right and true proportion to God and the world and other people.

Man's soul, thus redeemed and restored, returns to the right relation to God which is depicted in the second chapter of Genesis: he is in God's garden, and knows that he is there to dress it and keep it. He has indeed tasted of the tree of the knowledge of good and evil and developed his faculties in a multitude of wrong ways, and has made his way in the world, exploiting the resources of the earth and exploiting other men in defiance of the Law of God. For this he has incurred death in manifold ways, has earned the wages of Sin, has known despair and perdition.

Yet at last the Seed of the Woman has bruised the Serpent's head, and has brought Man back to peace with God, back into the garden, there to taste of the Tree of Life, in the midst of the garden; and ' the leaves of the tree are for the healing of the nations ', ' and there shall be no curse any more; for the throne of God and of the Lamb shall be therein; and His servants shall serve Him, and they shall see His face, and His name shall be on their foreheads ' (Rev. 22. 2–4).

F. E. Coggin, *The Second Story of Genesis as Literature*. Heffer, Cambridge, 1938.

C. S. Lewis, *Perelandra*. John Lane, 1943. (Macmillan.)

CHAPTER IV

' *Abraham believed God* '

THE STORIES IN THE BOOK OF GENESIS

WE will now continue with the Book of Genesis in a much more rapid and summary way. We have said that the real study of the Bible consists not in collecting information about the books, the writers, and the course of the history, but in learning, so far as we can, what it was that the writers really intended to say. But to do that, we need to learn what the scholars have to tell us about the dates of the books.

The Book of Genesis, with the rest of the Pentateuch, was not finally completed till the post-exilic period. As therefore we are concerned in this chapter with the parts of the books which were written before the Exile, while the Israelites were still in Canaan, we shall leave on one side for the present all that belongs to the so-called ' priestly document ' (P) including for instance the whole Book of Leviticus, which contains most of the post-exilic law of sacrifice ; we shall limit ourselves to the documents called J and E, which took shape during the period of the Monarchy, perhaps from about the time of the prophet Elijah onwards.

THE PERIOD OF THE JUDGES AND THE KINGS

The history of the period during which the Israelites were in Canaan is told in order in the books of Joshua, Judges, 1 and 2 Samuel, and 1 and 2 Kings. For the ordinary modern reader, this is much the simplest and most straight-forward part of the Old Testament, because it presents us with a continuous history, covering eight centuries, more or less, down to the year 562 B.C. Obviously the concluding part of 2 Kings was written after the Fall of Jerusalem; but the rest was mostly written before. There are in these books plenty of problems for the critical historian. But the narrative as a whole is in the full light of history; it is of interest to find that in the Mesopotamian clay-tablets there is an Assyrian record of the battle of Karkar, when the forces of King Ahab formed part of an allied army which fought the Assyrian army in 854 B.C., and Sennacherib's own account of his invasion of Judah which is recorded in 2 Kings 18 and 19.

It was during this period that the J and E documents were written; and they include most of the familiar and well-loved stories of the Book of Genesis. We must then begin by asking ourselves what was happening in Israel's spiritual history during this period, and what was the faith by which the faithful Israelite was living. What did they believe about God and God's dealings with them?

We can answer, without any doubt at all, that they would have expressed their faith somewhat thus: 'We believe that Yahweh our God redeemed (delivered) us from oppression in Egypt, in the days of Moses, with a mighty hand and an outstretched arm; that He brought us to Sinai (or Horeb) and there made His Covenant with us, that we might be His people and He our God: that after a period in the desert He brought us into the Land of Canaan and has given us possession of it: that we are to live as His people, obeying His commandments, and trusting Him to accomplish His good purpose with us in the future.'

Such was the faith which the Israelites brought with them

from the desert. But in Canaan they were learning for the first time the arts of agriculture, and we begin to hear of the ' corn and the wine and the oil '. They did not exterminate the Canaanites (we are told this plainly in Judges 1. 27–end) but lived among them. Necessarily therefore they learned from the Canaanites also the appropriate religious rites associated with ploughing and sowing and harvest. Hence came a great spiritual conflict, which could not be escaped, between the faith of Yahweh the God of Israel and the nature-religions of Canaan, the cults of the Baalim and the Ashtaroth. The issue was this: Would the final result be that Israel's religion would be fundamentally Canaanite, with fragments of the religion of Yahweh mixed in with it, so that Yahweh would become in effect one of the gods of the land, one of the Baals? Or would it be that the faith of Yahweh who had redeemed them out of Egypt would remain dominant, and would incorporate into itself the positive elements of the Canaanite religion, so that He and He alone would be acknowledged as Israel's God, and be worshipped both as the Redeemer and as the God of nature and Lord of the harvest, the giver of the corn and the wine and the oil?

Let us note that a similar conflict has had to be fought by God's people many times since. So it was in the Graeco-Roman world, when the Christian Church emerged from Judaism and went out into the world of the Roman Empire, where as St. Paul says there were ' gods many and lords many '; would Jesus Christ become one of the sages, or one of the pagan divinities, with Osiris and Mithra? Or would He be acknowledged as the only true Lord and Saviour, and the Church's faith be enriched with the treasures of Greek wisdom? So it is in the Church to-day in such a country as India, where the actual issue is whether there will appear a revised form of Hinduism, essentially Hindu in outlook, but with a selection of those elements in Christianity which appeal to Hindus, re-interpreted in the light of the Hinduism already held : or whether India is to accept the Christian faith and be baptized into Christ, while at the same time the essential Christian faith is seen through Indian eyes and re-expressed in an Indian way.

In the story of the Israelites in Canaan we see this sort of conflict being fought for the very first time. The situation in the early period is thus summarized by the editor of Judges (Judges 2. 11-23) and the summary is substantially true to the facts : that the people went after the Baalim and the Ashtaroth, forgetting their faith in Yahweh (2. 12-13) : that raids were made by the trans-Jordanian tribes on the fair cultivated lands (14-15) : then the LORD raised up a ' judge ' who rallied the tribes in the name of Yahweh (16, 18) ; but only for a time, for a relapse followed (19).

We are given a vivid description of the rising headed by Gideon in Judges 6. The Midianites invade the country and carry off the harvest (6. 3-4). Then in 6. 11 the call of the LORD comes to Gideon. He recalls the Deliverance from Egypt, and asks why Yahweh has seemingly cast them off (13). He is told to take action (16) ; he offers a sacrifice and receives encouragement (18-24). Then he destroys the altar of Baal, with the help of ten trusty men, by night because he dare not do it by day (25-7). In the morning the matter is inquired into (28-30), but Gideon's father stands by him (31-2). Then the Spirit of Yahweh comes on Gideon (34), and the rising of the tribes follows.

We must think of this conflict between the faith of Yahweh and the nature-religions as going on continuously throughout this long period, and of Samuel as a figure of the first importance in it, and of the establishment of the kingship in the person of Saul as a great event, for Saul was a great worshipper of Yahweh, even if he did not fulfil his early promise ; David carried out what Saul left unfulfilled. Yet the conflict was going on in every family and in every village and town ; and it reached a climax in the ministry of Elijah, who was faced with a recrudescence of paganism in the worship of the Tyrian Baal encouraged by Jezebel. In the great scene of the sacrifice on Carmel in 1 Kings 18 the issue is whether Yahweh or Baal is God. In the days of the prophet Hosea, as we shall see in chapter VI, the conflict is still going on.

THE STORIES OF ABRAHAM

It is in the light of this great conflict for the Faith that we must seek to understand the stories of Abraham, which may date from round about the time of Elijah. The stories about Abraham were traditional stories, and it is a fair inference that in the form in which we have them they were told by word of mouth before they were written down, probably in the ' schools of the prophets ', of which we hear in connexion with Elisha. As we read these stories, we cannot fail to see how the writer (or narrator) is holding up Abraham to his hearers as a pattern of faith in Yahweh.

In Gen. 12. 1, Abraham receives God's call to leave his home, and set out for a far country, trusting God :

Now the LORD said unto Abram, ' Get thee out of thy country, and from thy kindred, and from thy father's house, unto the land that I will show thee : and I will make of thee a great nation, and I will bless thee, and make thy name great ; and be thou a blessing : and I will bless them that bless thee, and him that curseth thee will I curse ; and in thee shall all the families of the earth be blessed.' (Gen. 12. 1–3.)

Abraham believes, and obeys, and receives God's blessing. We do right to put side by side with the story in Genesis the

magnificent commentary on it in Heb. 11. 8–16 which begins,
' By faith Abraham, when he was called, obeyed to go out to
a place which he was to receive for an inheritance ; and he
went out, not knowing whither he went . . .'

In Gen. 13 we have the story of Abraham and Lot. There
is not room in the land for them both ; ' and Lot lifted up
his eyes, and beheld all the plain of Jordan, that it was well
watered everywhere, before the LORD destroyed Sodom and
Gomorrah ' (13. 10) and chose to go to Sodom ; but ' the
men of Sodom were wicked and sinners before the LORD
exceedingly ' (13. 13). In other words, Lot ' went Canaanite '.
In the sequel (chapters 18 and 19), the judgement of the
LORD falls on Sodom for its sin, which is luridly described ;
Lot only escapes with his life, and his wife does not escape
(19. 26). Meanwhile Abraham remains on the hill-tops,
communing with God (13. 14–18 ; 18. 1).

The faith of Abraham throughout these chapters is faith
in a God who makes promises concerning the future (12. 1–3,
7–8 ; 13. 14–18 ; 15. 1–6, and the rest of that chapter) ;
we see how fundamental to the Old Testament is the conception of God as working out his purpose in history.
Hence comes the preoccupation of Abraham with the birth
of a son, his anxiety over the barrenness of Sarah (15. 2–3),
and his willingness to obtain children by Hagar (16. 1–2),
though he is told that God's purpose is not to be worked
out this way (15. 4). Then in chapter 18 comes the word
of the LORD that Sarah, in spite of her age, shall bear a son
(18. 10). Sarah mocks at this, not believing that it can be
true ; but she is assured ' Is anything too hard for the
LORD ? ' (18. 14). This word ' too hard for ' (*pala*) is one
of the great words of the Bible ; it comes again in the
word *niphla'oth*, which is variously translated as ' wondrous
works ', ' mighty acts ', ' miracles ', &c., and denotes the

action of God in bringing to pass things which are humanly impossible, too great for human power. The phrase of Gen. 18. 14 comes again in Jer. 32. 17: 'there is nothing too hard for thee', and again in verse 27; it lies behind the word of the angel at the Annunciation, Luke 1. 37, 'for no word of God shall be void of power', and our Lord's words in Mark 10. 27, 'for with God nothing shall be impossible', where He is speaking of 'miracles of grace'. We can compare His words about believing prayer in Mark 11. 22–4. Nothing is 'too hard for the LORD' if it is according to His will.

Sarah's child is born. Then comes the supreme trial of Abraham's faith, when God 'proves' or 'tempts' or 'tests' him by the command to offer the son in sacrifice:

And it came to pass after these things, that God did prove Abraham, and said unto him, 'Abraham'; and he said, 'Here am I'. And he said, 'Take now thy son, thine only son, whom thou lovest, even Isaac, and get thee into the land of Moriah; and offer him there for a burnt offering upon one of the mountains which I will tell thee of.' (Gen. 22. 1–2.)

Compared with such a demand, a command to the father to surrender his own life would be a small thing. The command to offer up the son of the promise, with whom the whole future lies, seems the complete contradiction of the Purpose of God in which he has set his faith. Here again we have the thought of God's purpose working through something humanly impossible.

If we turn to the commentary on this story in Heb. 11. 17–19, we find this point brought out. 'By faith Abraham being tried offered up Isaac; yea, he that had gladly received the promises was offering up his only-begotten son, even he to whom it was said "In Isaac shall thy seed be called";

accounting that God is able to raise up even from the dead; from whence he did also in a parable receive him back.' The reference to the Resurrection is here intended, as it seems, to take our thoughts to our Lord Himself, to whom it became clear that the divine will for Him was that He should offer Himself in sacrifice, content to surrender His life in the prime of life, with His life-work seemingly unaccomplished and seemingly ending in rejection by the people to whom He came and the complete failure of His mission; content to surrender Himself and His whole vocation and mission into the Father's hands. Such was the road which our Lord Himself was content to tread. The way of God's will led to something humanly impossible. He was vindicated when God raised Him from the dead.

And so Abraham in the story is called by God to make a supreme sacrifice, an act of complete and entire worship, trusting God in the dark, committing everything to Him: 'not my will but Thine be done'. While God did not in the end demand this sacrifice to be made, that which He did demand was the entire willingness to make the offering. Such is the meaning of the story as the writer tells it; and because this and nothing less is the true and original meaning therefore we, in interpreting it, may and must look onward to the self-giving of our Lord, in whose case no offering of a substitute was possible. Hence we may and must find the *final* answer to Isaac's question ' Where is the lamb for a burnt-offering?', and Abraham's reply ' God will provide himself the lamb for a burnt-offering, my son ' (22. 7–8), in the words of John 1. 29 ' Behold the Lamb of God that taketh away the sin of the world.'

The thought of the carrying-on of God's purpose, attested by His promise, comes again in Genesis chapter 24, where Abraham's servant goes in his name to find a wife for Isaac.

This whole chapter is dominated by the determination of the servant to submit the whole affair to God's guiding (see 24. 12–14, 21, 26–7). When he has told his story to Rebekah's parents, they acknowledge the hand of the LORD in it all: 'Behold, the thing proceedeth from the LORD: we cannot speak unto thee bad or good' (24. 50). It was impossible after this to discuss the matter on grounds of what might seem humanly desirable or expedient.

To the story of Abraham, Sarah, and Isaac, there is added the episode of Hagar, the mother of Ishmael. Twice over Hagar is sent away into the desert; first when Sarah is jealous of her handmaid who has conceived (16. 5–6), and again after Isaac has been born, and Hagar has mocked at him (21. 9–10). Yet each time we are told that God did not forget poor Hagar; in 16. 7–13 the Angel of the LORD finds her in the wilderness, and tells her that God has a purpose for Ishmael also, and (very movingly) again in 21. 14–21, after the water in the bottle is spent, and the mother has left the child to die:

And the water in the bottle was spent, and she cast the child under one of the shrubs. And she went, and sat her down over against him a good way off, as it were a bowshot: for she said, 'Let me not look upon the death of the child.' And she sat over against him, and lift up her voice, and wept. And God heard the voice of the lad: and the angel of God called to Hagar out of heaven, and said unto her, 'What aileth thee, Hagar? fear not; for God hath heard the voice of the lad where he is.' . . . And God opened her eyes, and she saw a well of water; and she went, and filled the bottle with water, and gave the lad drink. (Gen. 21. 15–19.)

It would have been easy and natural for the writer, whose whole narrative turned on the working out of the Purpose through Isaac and not through Ishmael, to treat Hagar with indifference, as cast-off and rejected : was not Hagar's son Ishmael the ancestor of tribes who were constantly at war with Israel, and on whom God's vengeance was many times invoked (cf. Ps. 83. 6, 13–end) ? But this is precisely what this writer will not do. He will not have his readers (or hearers) think of the surrounding pagan tribes as having nothing to do with God, or God with them.

It is indeed possible that earlier versions of this story had been current, in which the rejected mother and son had been treated with contempt. If that be so, our author has modified an earlier version of the story. In the case of two other stories, one is strongly tempted to think that this was the case : these are the two instances in which Abraham, going temporarily into a foreign country, passes off Sarah as his sister (Gen. 12. 10–20 and chapter 20 : cf. the same story told of Isaac, 26. 1–11). The fact that these stories were handed down at all is so strange, that it would seem highly probable that their *motif* in their original form, was to show how clever God's chosen servants had been in outwitting the foreigner. If this be the case, the writers of our stories have altered them very significantly ; but in any case the meaning which they have put into the stories remains the same.

Of the three stories in which the wife is passed off as a sister, the second is the most detailed and interesting. Abraham is in the land ruled by Abimelech. God warns Abimelech in a dream not to touch Sarah (20. 3) ; he protests his integrity and innocence (5) ; God acknowledges this, and says that He Himself has withheld him from sinning in the matter (6). Abimelech is greatly afraid, and calls Abraham and reproves him severely for putting him in danger of sinning so great a sin (9). Many centuries later, the writer of one of the books of the Apocrypha, the

D

Prayer of Manasses, could not imagine it possible for Abraham, Isaac, and Jacob to sin. But our writer in the Book of Genesis was wiser. He did not think of the saints as like the sham saints in our stained-glass windows, but as real men of flesh and blood, who were strong so long as they believed in God, but were weak and sinful when their faith in Him failed. In this instance Abraham shows up as morally inferior to the pagan chieftain. What does the writer intend to say to his contemporaries? Perhaps something like this: 'When you go to Egypt or Syria, do not imagine that you have gone out of the LORD's sight or beyond the range of His moral Law; and do not despise the people there, because you belong to the LORD's chosen people. You yourself are on trial: and maybe there will be in them a moral goodness which will put you to shame.' Have not we in England a proverbial saying that one leaves the Ten Commandments behind when one goes east of Suez?

THE STORIES OF JACOB AND JOSEPH

Of Isaac himself we are told little, but much about Jacob. Here we are again brought up against the question whether the stories existed once in an earlier form; indeed, in some instances (e.g. chapters 34, 38), it does appear that the earlier form of the story has remained 'unrevised'. We must not, indeed, blame our writer for the deceit which Jacob practises on Esau in stealing his blessing in chapter 27, for he tells the story in such a way as to make us feel sorry for Esau. Again, it can be pointed out that Esau in the story simply does not care about the birthright, the vocation, and the promise (27. 25, 29–34), and gets what he really cares about, an open-air life, chieftainship, wealth of flocks and herds; while Jacob, mean and deceitful though he is, yet is presented as a character who is ennobled through suffering. The man who wrote the words : ' I will not leave thee, until I have done that which I have spoken to thee of ' (28. 15), and who spoke of Jacob's sense of fear after he had seen such a dream (' Surely the Lord is in this place and I knew it not,' verse 16) —knew what he was talking about : and the story of Jacob's wrestling with God at Peniel (32. 24–30) is the work of one who had learnt deep lessons of prayer. There is justification, then, for the interpretation of the story of Jacob as that of the slow formation of a godly character, in a man whose youth had been crafty and selfish. It may be, then, that the selfishness of his vow to God in 28. 20–2 (if God will be with Jacob, and look after him and bring him home in peace, then Jacob will take the LORD for his God, and will duly pay Him his tithe) is intended by the writer as part of a character-study. It certainly contrasts very sharply with the faith of Abraham. Jacob in Syria is a highly unattractive figure ; and he can attribute to divine inspiration (31. 11) the experiments in sheep breeding by which the increase of the flocks was secured to him, at Laban's expense.

The long story of Joseph has been handed down, as it seems, in two versions which have been incompletely harmonized ; was it Midianites (37. 28, 36) or was it Ishmaelites (37. 27, 28) who carried Joseph down into Egypt ? The inference from the existence of two inconsistent versions of the story is that it was a story told by various narrators, and much in demand. There are certain highly important spiritual truths which the story as we have it conveys. There is Joseph's moral uprightness, when exposed to great temptation, alone in a pagan land : ' how then could I do this great wickedness and sin against God ' (39. 8–9) ; there is his patient endurance of undeserved suffering, without losing heart (39. 20–23, 40. 23). Above all, the climax to which the story leads up, is the truth of God's providence over-ruling the selfish acts of evil men (45. 5–8 and again 50. 20 : 'As for you, ye meant much evil against me ; but God meant it for good, to bring to pass as it is this day, to save much people alive ').

Finally, through this story, as through the whole book, runs the 'red thread' of the Divine Purpose ; God's blessing given to Abraham is continued to Isaac and Jacob, and His promise works itself out in the story, which brings us to the ancestors of the twelve tribes of the children of Israel.

Such were the stories which were told to the Israelite people in the prophetic schools or at the shrines. We have been thinking of the spiritual and moral lessons which the narrators intended to convey. Yet it would be unfair to them to say that their chief aim in telling the stories was didactic and moralistic ; if it had been, the stories would have been dull. Rather we should think that they loved the traditional stories and strove to tell them well ; but in proportion as their minds were full of faith in the LORD God of Israel, and of the conviction that His service was the one thing that mattered, the stories which they told reflected their faith.

F. D. Maurice, *Patriarchs and Lawgivers of the Old Testament.* 1851.

G. E. Phillips, *The Transmission of the Faith.* Lutterworth Press, 1946.

On the conflict with pagan religion (cf. p. 36) :

G. E. Phillips, *The Old Testament in the World Church.* Lutterworth Press, 1942. (Esp. p. 95 and onward.)

CHAPTER V

'Thy wonders of old time'

THE EXODUS AND THE SUBSEQUENT HISTORY

AFTER Genesis comes Exodus. Here we have the narrative
of the events on which the existence of Israel as the People
of God was based. They believed that Yahweh their God,
whom they felt and knew to be truly God in a sense in
which the deities of the surrounding nations were not, had
taken action in delivering them out of Egypt and uniting
them to Himself by a Covenant. This meant something
very different from speaking of Him as ' father ', as idolaters
did (Jer. 2. 27), thereby asserting that there was a bond of
quasi-natural kinship between the god and his tribe, and
the tribal deity was as it were ' one of the family '. On
such a view, an ordinary defeat in war might be a sign of the
god's momentary displeasure ; but a really crushing defeat
would mean that he had been overpowered. In fact the
tribal god was the personification of the genius of the tribe,
like the Britannia on an English penny. But Yahweh the
God of Israel was totally different from this. It was indeed
the constant temptation of the Israelites to drop into pagan
conceptions of Him. But the acid test came, as we shall
see, when His people suffered crushing defeat and national
ruin, and the prophets said that He Himself was punishing
His People for their sin. It was not till this lesson of the
absolute difference between the true God and the false gods

47

had been thoroughly learnt that the word Father could come back again, and be used as it is for instance in Psalm 103 :

> Yea, like as a father pitieth his own children,
> Even so is the LORD merciful unto them that fear Him,

and in the New Testament.

This sense of the reality of God is bound up with His action in history. It was not merely that the Israelites had a somewhat more exalted conception of Him than the other nations had of their gods. If that were all, we might expect to find the prophets exhorting the surrounding tribes to think more nobly of their gods, and saying that all the gods whom men worship are only names for the One. But they do not ; they say Yahweh is true God and the others are not, and they constantly refer back to the deliverance from Egypt (see, e.g., among the earliest prophets, Amos 2. 10, 3. 1–2 ; Hos. 2. 15, 11. 1 ; Mic. 6. 3–4). It is not that God does not care about other nations—for, says Amos, it is Yahweh who has brought up the Philistines from Caphtor (probably Crete), and the Syrians from Kir, as well as Israel from the land of Egypt (Amos 9. 7)—it is that Israel stands in a unique position, in being called to belong to Him who is the true God. In Deuteronomy the point is made and pressed home that the faith of Israel is an altogether unique fact among the religions of the world, with no parallel anywhere else :

For ask now of the days that are past, which were before thee, since the day that God created man upon the earth, and from the one end of heaven unto the other, whether there hath been any such thing as this great thing is, or hath been heard like it ? Did ever people hear the voice of God speaking out of the midst of the fire, as thou hast heard, and live ? Or hath God assayed to go and take him a nation from the midst of another nation, by temptations,

by signs, and by war, and by a mighty hand and a stretched out
arm, and by great terrors, according to all that Yahweh your God
did for you in Egypt before your eyes? Unto thee it was shewed,
that thou mightest know that Yahweh he is God: there is none
else beside him (Deut. 4. 32–5).

A faith such as the faith of old Israel in the God who
redeemed it out of Egypt, or that of the Church in the Son
of God come down from heaven, who was born as true
man on earth, was crucified when Pontius Pilate was pro-
curator of Judea, and rose victorious from death, makes an
appeal to history which demands to be tested by the best
methods of historical investigation. Only so can we answer
the very legitimate question, whether these alleged events
are not merely legendary; and if in fact the gospel records
of the resurrection of our Lord can claim to be treated as
the testimony of honest men to an amazing series of events,
it is only historical criticism that can prove this. And the
Christian faith does depend on the answer, as St. Paul shows
in 1 Cor. 15. 14–17. 'If Christ hath not been raised, then
is our preaching vain, your faith also is vain. Yea, and we
are found false witnesses of God, because we testified of
God that he raised up Christ.' If it were proved beyond
all reasonable doubt that Jesus of Nazareth never existed,
but is a pure myth created by the religious needs of the
world of that day; or that He was simply a teacher or
religious reformer and no more, and that the whole claim
that He was Messiah and Saviour was the invention of the
Christian Church; or that the reliable historical record ends
with His death, and the whole story of the resurrection is
the product of wishful thinking on the part of disciples who
dare not face facts—if any of these things were proved
beyond reasonable doubt, the Christian Faith would be at
an end. For it stands on the assertion: 'Blessed be the

Lord God of Israel, for he hath visited and redeemed his people.'

The same must apply to the Old Testament, since there also it is proclaimed that God took action in a series of events in history.

THE EXODUS OF ISRAEL FROM EGYPT

The story of Israel as a nation begins with the Exodus from Egypt and the Covenant at Horeb. We do not need to take seriously the hypothesis that the whole narrative is mere myth, and there never was any Exodus at all; the historical evidence is too strong for that to be possible. What we do need to treat seriously is the hypothesis that there was indeed an Exodus under a great leader called Moses, but that in the earliest times this was interpreted and understood in a purely ' natural ' way, and that it was the writers of the eighth century who first saw in it the work of such a God as the prophets believed in. On this hypothesis there was no true act of God in the Exodus.

We are now asking the question, ' Of what character is the Exodus story, in the form in which it has come down to us ? ' If it was a traditional story that existed in an early form, and was radically changed by the prophets so that it came to mean something entirely different, we should expect some elements of the original story to persist in the records after the transformation had taken place. Originally, on this view, the Exodus-story will have been a folk-tale, telling of the glory and prowess of Israel's God, His might in overthrowing His enemies, and the prowess of His people too as they fight their battles under his leadership and protection ; some traces of this view will assuredly persist in the story, after it has been re-written.

Certainly the power of Yahweh is shown in the repeated

plagues of Egypt, and above all in the overwhelming of the Egyptian army in the Red Sea. But we shall expect to hear of Israel's prowess also. Do we find this? Instead, we find Moses' act in killing the Egyptian and rescuing the Hebrew (Exod. 2. 11–12) not accepted with gratitude as by a noble race longing for its deliverance (2. 13–14). Moses at Horeb receives the revelation of God's Name, and the call to go and deliver Israel (3. 1–14); yet Moses, the great Moses, shrinks from the task and does all he can to escape from it (4. 1–17), before at last he goes. The first plea to Pharaoh, that he let the people go, produces only an increase of the people's burdens, and they tell Moses that they do not want His promised deliverance; they are better as they are, and prefer to remain in slavery (5. 21). After this, the Plagues of Egypt follow (three narratives which originally contained 8, 5 and 5 plagues respectively, having been combined in chapters 6–12), culminating in the Passover and the passage of the Red Sea. This is the very hour of deliverance; yet the Israelites are not represented as a band of brave men fighting their way through to freedom, nor as dying like the Spartans at Thermopylae, but as a herd of helpless fugitives, caught between the sea and their enemies, and expecting next morning a fate worse than death, and saying to Moses,

Because there were no graves in Egypt, hast thou taken us away to die in the wilderness? . . . Is not this the word that we spake unto thee in Egypt, 'Let us alone, that we may serve the Egyptians'? (14. 11, 12.)

Then the marvel happened. If we follow Phythian-Adams' exposition in his book *The Call of Israel*, the sea receded as it has been known to do often at times of volcanic eruption, and a few hours later came back in a tremendous tidal wave: so it was that Israel went across on dry land, and standing safe on the eastern bank saw their enemies engulfed as they tried to follow. The sight which they saw is recorded in the very ancient ballad of Exod. 15:

> I will sing to the LORD, for he hath triumphed gloriously,
> The horse and his rider hath he thrown into the sea.

This is nothing even remotely like the ordinary patriotic tale, which glorifies at once the tribal god, the heroic leader, and the people. There is emphasis on the slowness even of the great leader to accept his mission, and on the servility and timidity of the people, entirely unlike the praises of their prowess that we get in the Song of Deborah in Judges 5; and this attitude on the part of the people can be no later addition to the story, for it is on the helplessness of the people in the hour of their deliverance that the whole record hangs. We may remind ourselves that the same feature appears in the narratives of our Lord's passion, where we are told, not how the faithful disciples stood by their Lord to the last, but how 'they all forsook him and fled', and one of them betrayed Him and one disowned Him publicly. Here the apostles, who are proclaiming to the world that Christ died to save sinners, are heard confessing their own share in the common sin. Both in the New Testament and in the Old Testament instance, when the usual human tendency to self-congratulation and self-praise is thus reversed, the inference is that some real event has happened to produce such a phenomenon.

In chapters 4–11 of the Book of Deuteronomy, written towards the end of the pre-exilic period, we get a series of magnificent homilies on the Exodus and the vocation of Israel which results from it; we have already quoted (pp. 48–9 above) some verses from chapter 4. Here is another notable piece of commentary:

Thou art a holy people unto Yahweh thy God: Yahweh thy God hath chosen thee to be a peculiar people to himself, above all peoples that are on the face of the earth. Yahweh did not set his love upon you nor choose you, because ye were more in number than any people: for ye were the fewest of all peoples: but because Yahweh loveth you, and because he would keep the oath which he sware unto your fathers, hath Yahweh brought you out with a mighty hand, and redeemed you out of the house of bondage, from the hand of Pharoah king of Egypt. (Deut. 7. 6–8.)

The nation which Yahweh chose to be His people was a small and insignificant nation. (Here we may note that the figure of 'six hundred thousand men that drew sword, besides women and children' in Exod. 12. 37 belongs to a later version of the story as told by a post-exilic writer; the actual number may have been a few thousands all told.) The general sense of the Deuteronomic interpretation is true to that of the narrative in Exodus, where the LORD God is praised for the amazing deliverance at the Red Sea and Moses the great leader is shown as His unworthy human instrument, and the people as the unworthy objects of his mercy.

Nor did Israel make up for the smallness of its numbers by the high quality of its devotion. Repeatedly Israel in the wilderness is found 'murmuring against Moses and against God' (Exod. 15. 24; 16. 2, 7: Num. 20. 2–13). Here is another Deuteronomic commentary:

Thou shalt remember all the way that Yahweh thy God hath led thee these forty years in the wilderness, that he might humble thee, to prove thee, to know what was in thine heart, whether thou wouldest keep his commandments, or no. And he humbled thee, and suffered thee to hunger, and fed thee with manna, which thou knewest not, neither did thy fathers know, that he might make thee know that man doth not live by bread alone, but by every thing that proceedeth out of the mouth of Yahweh doth man live. (Deut. 8. 2–3.)

The rest of this chapter, and the following chapters, enlarge on the theme that it was the same after the people entered Canaan.   There was to be the danger

lest when thou hast eaten and art full, and hast built goodly houses and dwelt therein, and when thy herds and thy flocks multiply, and thy silver and thy gold is multiplied, and all that thou hast is multiplied, then thine heart be lifted up and thou forget Yahweh thy God, which brought thee forth out of the land of Egypt, out of the house of bondage. (Deut. 8. 12–14.)

Israel having received its vocation had still to make good.

THE COVENANT

To return now from Deuteronomy to Exodus : we read in chapter 24 of a solemn sacrifice with communion feast, at which the Covenant of Yahweh with Israel was ratified and sealed, and Israel was consecrated to Him.

The ordinary sort of ' covenant' was a bargain or pact between one man and another, by which the two parties entered on a new relation, with reciprocal rights and duties. Such is the covenant of Jacob and Laban in Gen. 31. 44–5. Here the two parties stand on an equal footing.   But when God makes a covenant with men, the two parties do not stand on an equal footing.   Such a covenant cannot therefore be thought of as a species of bargain, but must rest on the gracious mercy of God, condescending to enter on a relation with men, and admitting men to a special relation to Him. It is therefore entirely misleading and wrong to represent His Covenant with Israel as an agreement or contract, so that if man fails to perform his duty to God, the Covenant is

broken. On the contrary : the Covenant stands, even when
Israel sins, because its basis is the free act of the divine Love,
as in Deut. 7. 6–8, quoted on page 53 above. Another
expression of the idea is the relation of Bridegroom and
Bride, which we meet in the prophet Hosea (see p. 66 below) ;
as Hosea still loved his unfaithful wife, so Yahweh still loves
sinful Israel.

The Covenant at Horeb looks forward to the New Covenant promised in Jer. 31. 31–4, and fulfilled in the New
Covenant which was ratified by our LORD's sacrifice ; see
pp. 102–3 below. Other divine Covenants spoken of in the
Old Testament are God's covenant with ' all flesh ', in the
story of Noah after the Flood, Gen. 9. 1–17 (see p. 89
below), and the covenant of circumcision, which God makes
with Abraham in Gen. 17.

There are also the Covenants with God made by men on
two important occasions in the Old Testament history, when
men bound themselves to God's service in some particular
way. These two historical occasions are the Covenant
of Josiah, when the Deuteronomic Law was accepted
(2 Kings 23. 3 ; p. 74 below), and the Covenant of Ezra's
Reform (Neh. 9. 38 ; pp. 114–16 below).

With the Covenant at Horeb is associated the giving of
the Law : of the Ten Commandments, Exod. 20. 1–17, and
of a collection of laws which belong to the pre-exilic period,
Exod. 20. 22 to the end of chapter 23. These laws evidently
belong to the life of an agricultural community. After what
we have said, it will not seem surprising that these laws really
date from the time when the narrative was written : for as
the Israelites commemorated the Deliverance from Egypt
year by year at the Passover, as being the foundation on
which their own life as Yahweh's people rested, so they
saw the Covenant at Horeb as related to their own life in

Canaan. Similarly and for the same reason, in Exod. 25–31 and 35–40 and the Book of Leviticus, we have other laws, of post-exilic date, but all treated as belonging to the Mosaic Covenant.

THE HISTORY OF ISRAEL IN CANAAN

We have been dealing with the acts of God in history, by which Israel was constituted as the people of the LORD. We must now treat, very briefly and summarily, of His continuing presence and action throughout the subsequent history. For this Bible history is very different from the ordinary style of history in our own history-books, and we need to see what sort of history it is.

Throughout this history, God is represented as taking the initiative. In Num. 9. 15–23 and 10. 33–6 we are told that their movements in the desert were regulated by His orders from day to day. He gives the word for them to cross the Jordan and enter Canaan (Joshua 1. 1–9). Before the assault on Jericho, Joshua sees a vision of the Captain of the LORD's Host, with His sword drawn in His hand (5. 13–15). So it is throughout. In the Book of Judges, the LORD raises up the Judges (i.e. ' national leaders ') (Judges 2. 16). He calls Gideon (6. 12). His angel appears to Manoah and his wife (13. 2–25), to announce the birth of Samson. Samuel is born (1 Sam. 1), in answer to his mother's prayer : in 1 Sam. 3. 1–10 He gives His personal call to the child Samuel.

To Samuel, and to every prophet after Samuel, the word of the LORD comes, as in 1 Sam. 9. 15 or 16. 1. By His word Saul is raised up to be king : but Saul fails to make good his vocation, and Samuel pronounces the LORD's judgement on him, 1 Sam. 13. 13–14 and 15. 10–11, 22–31 : ' thou hast rejected the word of the LORD, and the LORD hath rejected thee from being king over Israel'. By His word Samuel anoints the youthful David (16. 1–13). Every prophet, after Samuel, is sent by the LORD to speak His word; in every case He is represented as taking the initiative. When David sins over the matter of Bathsheba, the LORD sends Nathan to David to convict him of his sin (2 Sam. 12. 1–15). Solomon seeks and receives His blessing (1 Kings 3. 4–15); but he also misses his vocation (1 Kings 11. 1–13), and in his son's reign occurs the schism of Israel and Judah. Rehoboam acts foolishly (12. 1–14), and Jeroboam wickedly in setting up the rival sanctuaries with the Golden Calves at Bethel and Dan (12. 25–33); yet the thing was 'of the LORD' (12. 15 and 21–4).

After this in the Book of Kings, a judgement is recorded on each king in turn, as e.g. in 1 Kings 15. 3, Abijam's heart 'was not perfect with the LORD his God, as was the heart of David his father'; but while his son Asa 'did right in the eyes of the LORD' (verses 11–15), all the kings of the northern kingdom 'walked in the way of Jeroboam, and in his sin wherewith he made Israel to sin'. In 722 B.C. came the Fall of Samaria (2 Kings 17. 1–6); and in 17. 7–23 the historian gives a summary indictment of the sins of the people, which brought on them this terrible calamity. This subject, however, we must reserve till the next chapter.

THE BIBLE HISTORY

What sort of history is this? It is very different from our ordinary history-books, in that it deals with the history from the point of view of God's Purpose and God's dealing with His people. But every historian treats his history from some point of view. There are specialized histories, such as books of naval history, or of the history of social and economic conditions, or of church history. The textbooks of English history which I read when I was young had for their dominant idea the greatness of the English people. Every historian is bound to select the events which appear to him to be significant; a mere catalogue of events will be meaningless, for the events need to be interpreted.

If then the Biblical history interprets the events from the point of view of God's Purpose, that ought to be the widest and most comprehensive point of view from which the events could possibly be interpreted; for if we believe in God, we believe that the real meaning of all events is what God means by them. But no human writer, not even a Biblical writer, can fully understand God's Purpose, and interpret it with full completeness; the Book of Kings gives a far less searching judgement on the events of this period and on the people than do the Prophets.

Yet there is this to be said. What you find depends on what you are looking for. The answers that you give depend on the questions to which you are seeking an answer. If you are asking the wrong questions, you cannot possibly find a right answer. And when we have said this, we see at once that—unless indeed the whole Biblical conception of Israel's vocation and the Biblical faith in God were one huge mistake—the writers were asking the right questions; they were seeking the right thing. If the Books of Kings were concerned with the history of political theory and practice in Israel, or its military history, or the development of its domestic architecture, they would be of little interest or value; for the Israelites had little to contribute in these respects, far less than contemporary Egypt, or Babylon. That which makes the history of Israel significant, and indeed of vital importance for us all, is Israel's vocation to be the People of God.

It is important to see, however, that the history is something more than the history of Israel's religion. There is not much in these books, for instance, about religious services, except at one point, where the dedication of the great temple at Jerusalem is described in detail in 1 Kings 6–8. There are references to various other sanctuaries, and various sacrifices; but there is no systematic account of the 'religious' life of the people, in the narrower sense of the word. Religion in the life of the people of God did not take the place of bread and butter. What is described in these books is not the religious side of life, but the ordinary common life of the People of God. The writers are seeking to show what God meant by that ordinary common life, as the Israelites lived it.

It is not strange then, if parts of the Bible are mean and sordid, such as the story of Gideon's descendants in Judges 8–9. But in Judges 13 there is a charming picture of Manoah and his good wife, who see a vision of the Angel of the LORD, and fear that this means that they are going to die; but they argue that God is being good to them, otherwise He would not have accepted a sacrifice from them (13. 22–3). David, the 'man after the LORD's own heart', shows astonishing generosity and nobility of heart; but the followers whom he collected at the Cave of Adullam were a very rough lot indeed; 'every one that was in distress, and every one that was in debt, and every one that was discontented, gathered themselves unto him, and he became captain over them; and there were with him about four hundred men' (1 Sam. 22. 2).

It is a story of real life. It belongs to other days than our own, but it speaks to us. It shows us God coming to meet men where they are. It deals with ordinary people, not specially with Leaders of Thought. The moral standards which we find in it are shocking to us at certain points, as

E

for instance the command to destroy the Amalekites (1 Sam.
15. 3) said to have been given to Saul, and carried out, except
as regards the king himself and some livestock; the complete extermination of some tribesmen by David for reasons
of policy (1 Sam. 27. 7–11); the massacre by David of
two-thirds of his Moabite prisoners-of-war (2 Sam. 8. 2).
We are not required to approve of those savage deeds, or
say that because they were done by people in the Bible they
were right; even though we may quite honestly distinguish
these acts of cruelty done in primitive times, and comparable
to the cruelty of boys to animals or at least to one another,
from the deliberate and calculating cruelty of the ancient
Assyrian army and that of the modern concentration
camp. These cruelties occur, as we should expect such acts
to occur in a story of real life; and side by side with them
there occur other acts of an astonishing graciousness, which
show how men whose moral standards are regarded by us
as primitive, were yet capable of great nobleness: such as
David's chivalry in sparing Saul's life (1 Sam. 24. 4–6;
26. 7–12) and his elegy over Saul and Jonathan (2 Sam. 1.
19–27). Note that in this last instance the singer of the
elegy has just put to death the bearer of the news.

The conception of divine revelation which is involved in
His action in history and His dealings with His chosen people
throughout their history is above all that of a God who is
real, who is truly God, who is to be feared. It made all the
difference whether an Israelite king thought of the people's
religion primarily as a means whereby his power over them
might be made secure, by playing on their superstitious
fears, and using their religious feelings to heighten the awe
they felt for himself; or whether he believed that he himself
was answerable for his own conduct to the God in whom
his people were expected to believe. It seems that David

grasped this point, when he confessed that, in lusting after Bathsheba and causing her husband's death, ' I have sinned against the LORD ' (2 Sam. 12. 13).

To believe in God as *real* is to believe in Him as interested in the actual life that men live : and this is a different thing from the abstract conception of correct ideas *about* God. Yet much that has been written about the Old Testament takes it for granted that divine revelation can consist in nothing else than the making-known of right ideas about God, as that He alone is God and no other divine beings exist : God has then been revealed when men have reached a definite monotheism.

But that is a Greek way, an intellectualist way, of regarding Revelation : it is not that of the Bible. Similarly in the Church we do not confess our faith in such terms as ' I believe that God is omnipotent and is at the same time Eternal Love : I believe that Jesus Christ exemplified for us the highest moral ideals and taught the brotherhood of man ' and so on. Our Creed is first an act of personal allegiance and self-committal : ' I believe *in* God.' Then, it describes the object of our belief in the simplest matter-of-fact terms : ' God the Father almighty, Maker of heaven and earth.' ' Jesus Christ, His only Son our Lord, Who was conceived by the Holy Ghost, born of the Virgin Mary, suffered under Pontius Pilate, crucified, dead, buried, rose the third day.' In these acts, through these events, God came to us.

So in the Old Testament God is known first of all as the real God, the God who is to be feared ; the other tribes have their tribal religions, but Israel's God is different. The conception of God's being and nature develops as the history goes on ; men learn to think rightly about Him, and they learn what are the demands of His spiritual service. We have seen something of this process of education going on in the stories in the Book of Genesis. But the supreme instruments of this teaching were the great prophets, to whom we come next.

On the interpretation of history :

R. G. Collingwood, *Autobiography*, Oxford, 1939. Penguin Books, 1944. (Chapter XI on ' Roman Britain '.) (O.U.P., N.Y.)

C. North, *The Old Testament Interpretation of History*. Epworth Press.

On the Exodus :

W. J. Phythian-Adams, *The Call of Israel*. Oxford University Press, 1934.

H. H. Rowley, *The Rediscovery of the Old Testament*. James Clark, 1945. (Ch. IV on ' The Meaning of History '.)

A continuous narrative of the history in :

W. J. Phythian-Adams, *The Fulness of Israel*. Oxford University Press, 1938. (From Ch. IV (p. 89) onwards.)

See also :

The Clarendon Bible, Vol. II : *From Moses to Elisha*, by T. H. Elliott-Binns. Oxford University Press, 1929.

CHAPTER VI

'O Israel, what shall I do unto thee?'

AMOS, HOSEA, ISAIAH, DEUTERONOMY

WE come now to a quite different style of writing: the poems, speeches, sermons, of the great prophets. The prophets are not only concerned with fore-telling the future, though they do this. They are engaged above all in interpreting the past and the present in the light of God's will. They hold up a mirror to Israel, in which Israel may see herself as she really is. As Amos puts it, they see the LORD standing beside the wall, with a plumb-line in His hand (Amos 7. 7). They rebuke not so much the private sins of individuals, as the common sin of which Israel is corporately guilty. They accuse the people first, of untrue and unreal worship of the LORD (chiefly Amos and Isaiah); second, of forsaking Him and going after the nature-religions of the Canaanites (chiefly Hosea); and third, of social iniquity and the oppression of the poor (all the prophets). We will take these three in turn, associating them respectively with Amos, Hosea, and Isaiah.

It is impossible to exaggerate the greatness of the prophets or the debt which our religion owes to them. So mighty is their stature, that some modern writers speak as if they and they alone were the creators of Israel's faith; as if the previous religion of Israel, before they appeared, had been no different from any of the neighbouring tribes. Certainly Israel would not have been Israel without them: in the working out of God's purpose they were His most notable instruments. But there were prophets before Amos, among whom Samuel, Nathan, and Elijah stand in the first rank. Nor do Amos and the others come forward as men proclaiming a new faith, unknown before : they are recalling the people to a faith which has been forgotten. They themselves stand within the Covenant, and continually appeal to the deliverance from Egypt in the Exodus as the foundation of Israel's existence. This remains true, even though in their utterances the old faith of Israel shines out with a brightness hitherto unknown.

A special difficulty, for the ordinary reader, arises from the way in which our ordinary Bibles are printed. The writings of the prophets are nearly all poetry, and need to be printed as such. Also, simple titles and sub-headings are needed, to indicate what the subject of each prophecy is. There is a further difficulty, especially in Isaiah, that in the collecting and editing of his prophecies a considerable amount of material of later date has come in, chiefly 13 and 14. 1–23 and 24–6 ; 36 and 37 are mostly the same as 2 Kings 18 and 19 ; and with chapter 40 we start on the work of the great prophet of the Exile whom we call the Second Isaiah.

Amos prophesied in the northern kingdom about 760 B.C. ; Hosea about ten or twenty years later. Isaiah belongs to Jerusalem ; his call was in 740 B.C., and his ministry continued till after Sennacherib's invasion in 701. Micah was his contemporary.

AMOS AND THE UNREAL WORSHIP OF THE LORD

Amos is the earliest of the writing prophets, and his style is so plain, simple and powerful, that it is easy for everyone to understand. He was a herdsman from Tekoah in Judah ; he tells us in 7. 14–15 how the LORD God had called him to go and prophesy in Israel, in the royal sanctuary at Bethel, in the northern kingdom (7. 10–13). As a countryman, he gives us some splendid pictures of the glory of God in nature (4. 13; 5. 8; 9. 6). He begins his prophecies with some stanzas declaring the judgement of the LORD on the surrounding peoples : the cities of Damascus, Gaza, Tyre, the tribes of Edom, Ammon, Moab ; then comes the turn of Judah, and finally of Israel (1. 2–2. 16). Above all, there is the sin of unreal worship; see 4. 4–5; 5. 4–8, 14. In 5. 16–20 we gather that the people are hopefully anticipating a 'Day of the LORD', when God will come to bless them and bring them joy, security, and peace. Amos says that the Day will be the very reverse of what they think. The Day will be darkness and not light; He hates, He despises their feasts, He will not have their sacrifices (5. 18, 22–3), so long as they think they can sin as they please, and then offer gifts to buy His favour. He has sent one warning after another, and they have not repented (4. 6–13).

Isaiah gives a similar message to Jerusalem, in chapter 1 and 2. 5–22; Micah in 6. 1–8. Perhaps the clearest statement of the principle is in Jeremiah chapter 7, where the prophet cries Woe on the people who put their trust in the Temple (7. 4). If they amend their lives and forsake their injustice in the law-courts, their cruelty to the helpless, and their worship of strange gods, all will be well (7. 5–7). But they think they can ' steal, murder, and commit adultery, and swear falsely, and burn incense to Baal, and walk after other gods ' and then come and stand before the LORD in His house, and say ' We are delivered ', that they may do all these abominations (7. 9–10). That is to make God's Temple into a ' den of robbers ' (7. 11). These last words were quoted by our Lord when He cleansed the Temple (Mark 11. 17); He meant (as Jeremiah meant) that the

Temple was being used like a cave which a bandit has among the mountains, where he retires for safety from pursuit after committing his robberies : or as we might say, like using gifts to religious purposes as a sort of celestial insurance policy against the more unpleasant consequences of wrong-doing. The prophets say that the LORD God will not have it. He is the living God, and His relation to His people is a personal relation. It is an insult to Him, therefore, when people come to offer Him sacrifices and make their prayers, as those who are buying His favour, in order to make things safe for themselves. The first lesson that man must learn about His relation to God is that he must fear Him, and treat as holy His holy Name, instead of profaning it by formalism and religious falsehood. 'Hallowed be thy Name.'

HOSEA AND THE WORSHIP OF OTHER GODS

Hosea's style, unfortunately, is as abrupt, jerky, and dis-connected as that of Amos is coherent and plain. The first three chapters, however, in which he tells us his life-story are mostly clear enough.

It is a story of an unhappy marriage. But did Hosea take a prostitute to be his wife at God's command, as 1. 2 seems to imply ? The expositors are mostly agreed that this was not so : Hosea was at first happily married to Gomer, and she afterwards proved unfaithful and committed adultery ; perhaps the second and third children were thus born. From this sad experience of his own broken marriage Hosea learnt that Yahweh loved Israel : He was Israel's true husband, and Israel His Bride ; and Israel had been unfaithful to Him, and had committed adultery against Him, in going after the nature-gods of Canaan. Since Hosea speaks in several places as if Israel had truly loved Yahweh when

He espoused her and made the Covenant with her in the
days of Moses, and describes her future return to Him,
after her period of chastisement, as a renewal of her first
love :

And she shall make answer there,
    As in the days of her youth,
    And as in the day when she came up out of the land of
        Egypt (2. 15)—

we can infer that Gomer had at one time truly loved Hosea.

Hosea, in grief over his ruined home, sent his wife away ;
after some years it seems that he found her serving as a
slave, for he tells us that he bought her back (3. 1, 2), and
kept her for a time deprived of conjugal rights. For he
loved his wife : and his human love and sorrow taught him
to apply these terms to God. 'When Israel was a child,
then I loved him, and called my son out of Egypt' (11. 1).
But Israel has gone after her ' other lovers ', and has forsaken
Him, though it was really He and not the Baalim who had
given her the corn and the wine and the oil (2. 8).   Therefore he must deal severely with her, and deprive her of the
gifts of civilization (2. 9–14), till she returns at last to
her true Husband (2. 7–8), with a renewal of her love
(2. 15).

Here, then, we have the beginning of a theme which runs
through the two Testaments.   Hosea sees Israel as Yahweh's
unfaithful Bride, who must be punished for her unchastity ;
and this theme is taken up by Jeremiah (2. 1–3 ; 3. 1–13 &c.)
and Ezekiel (chapter 16). We shall see how the prophets
of the Exile witness the execution of this sentence ; and then,
when Israel in exile has begun to learn repentance, there come
the promises of the Messianic days when she shall be the faithful wife (Isa. 54. 1–8 ; 62. 4–5) and Mother (Isa. 66. 10–13).

Our Lord, when He comes, speaks of Himself as the Bride-groom (the King's Son in the parable of the Wedding-Feast, Matt. 22. 2, and the Bridegroom in that of the Ten Virgins, Matt. 25. 1–13) ; and St. Paul works out at length the analogy of Christ the Bridegroom and Israel (the Church) as His Bride in Eph. 5. 22–33.

Was the word of the LORD spoken by His prophets success-ful, or did it fail ? Did the long conflict of the faith of Yahweh with the nature-religions of Canaan end in a victory or failure ? Failure, it would seem : for the northern kingdom came to an end in 722 B.C., and the author of 2 Kings 17. 7–23 pronounces judgement on it, for exactly the sins which Hosea denounced. The Ten Tribes dis-appeared from history.

Yet God's cause was not lost. It is never lost, so long as His servants are there, bearing witness to the truth. Nor did the northern tribes wholly disappear : for in Jeremiah there are repeated references to 'Israel' and 'Ephraim', esp. in Jer. 31, and when this prophet means Judah he says 'Judah', as in 31. 17, 31. Ezekiel in 37. 15–28 speaks of the reunion of Israel and Judah, first in the symbolism of a broken stick which is put together (37. 15–20) and then explicitly (verse 22). We should infer that when the people of Judah went into exile 130 years later, they found in Meso-potamia some of the northern tribes in whom the prophetic faith had remained alive.

ISAIAH AND SOCIAL INIQUITY

All the prophets speak of the sin of oppression of the poor. Large landowners get the poor into their power. There is sharp practice in buying farm produce ; in selling debtors into slavery; in unjust judgements in the law-courts ; in the eviction of farmers from their lands.

Some particularly notable passages are :

    1 Kings 21 (Naboth's vineyard).
    Amos 2. 6; 5. 10–12; 6. 3–6; 8. 4–6.
    Hosea 4. 1–2.
    Isaiah 1. 21–3; chapter 5; 10. 1–4.
    Micah 2. 1–2, 8–9; 3. 1–3, 9–12; 6. 8–12.

Yet none of the prophets can be called 'labour leaders' or 'champions of the working class'. They care about Israel as a whole, because Israel is the people of the LORD. They stand up for the poor because they form part of His Israel, and they denounce the sins of the rich and powerful because these are specially flagrant. They do not stand up for the rights of man in Rousseau's sense, but because man is precious in God's sight.

ISAIAH'S FAITH IN GOD

Those were peculiarly difficult times. In the days of Amos and Hosea the peril of Assyrian militarism had begun to be serious; these prophets foresaw and foretold defeat and deportation. In the days of Isaiah the peril had come very near. The people of Judah saw the destruction of the sister-kingdom, and throughout Isaiah's lifetime the 'war of nerves' was going on. The politicians of these small nations had a choice between a policy of 'appeasement' towards the Assyrian king, involving the payment of a heavy tribute (2 Kings 15. 19–20, 18. 13–16), with the threat of eventual deportation (cf. 2 Kings 18. 31–2), or a policy of seeking alliances, especially with Egypt (cf. Isa. 30. 1–5; 31. 1–3).

Isaiah in his later years became the foremost citizen of Jerusalem, and took a great part in politics. Yet he never became a partisan of either of the rival policies, but faced the issues in a serene faith in God as the Lord of history.

When he was still young, he denounced King Ahaz and his policy of appeasement (Isa. 7. 1–17). What manner of man Ahaz was may be gathered from 2 Kings 16; he called in the help of the Assyrian king against the kingdoms of Syria and Israel, and after he had destroyed Damascus Ahaz went to meet him there, and ordered an Assyrian altar to be built in the temple at Jerusalem, to offer sacrifices to the Assyrian god Asshur, as being evidently the strongest of all the gods (2 Kings 16. 10–16); and in order to placate Yahweh, offered up to Him his eldest son in sacrifice, as the costliest offering that he could make (16. 3).

It was no longer, as in the days of Hosea, a matter of standing up against the worship of the nature-gods of Canaan. Now, in terror of their lives, men were seeking the help of any gods in heaven or hell that might save them from disaster. It was in the midst of all this that Isaiah held to his faith in the LORD as the Lord of history. He saw the dreaded master of the irresistible military machine as an instrument in the LORD's hand, sent by Him to chastise His own sinful people (Isa. 10. 5–15); yet no more able to do anything without God's over-ruling control than an axe or a staff is able to assert itself against him who wields it (verse 15):

Ho, Assyrian, the rod of mine anger,
The staff in whose hand is mine indignation !
I will send him against a profane nation,
And against the people of my wrath will I give him a charge,
    To take the spoil,
    And to take the prey,
And to tread them down like the mire of the streets.
    Howbeit he meaneth not so,
    Neither doth his heart think so;
    But it is in his heart to destroy,
    And to cut off nations not a few. (10. 5–7.)

He boasts of his field-marshals: ' Are not my princes all of them kings ? '—and of the cities which he has sacked. But the last word lies with God:

> Wherefore it shall come to pass, that when the LORD hath performed His whole work upon mount Zion and on Jerusalem,
> I will punish the fruit of the stout heart of the king of Assyria,
> And the glory of his high looks.
> For he hath said, ' By the strength of my hand I have done it,
> And by my wisdom ; for I am prudent: . . .
> And my hand hath found as a nest the riches of the peoples ;
> And as one gathereth eggs that are forsaken,
> Have I gathered all the earth:
> And there was none that moved the wing,
> Or that opened the mouth, or chirped.'
> Shall the axe boast itself against him that heweth therewith ?
> Shall the saw magnify itself against him that shaketh it ?
> As if a rod should shake them that lift it up,
> Or as if a staff should lift up him that is not wood (10. 12–15).

The Hebrew prophets have given us the classical texts in all literature about national sin against God and His judgement on nations. To them we have continually to go back, to learn again what they have to say to us ; and the word of the LORD which they spoke is as fresh now as it was then—and as little heeded.

Just in one passage in the New Testament (and that a prophecy as great as any of the Old Testament prophecies for its splendour and terror) is the word of judgement brought up to date and applied to the sin of a corrupt industrial and commercial civilization. Revelation chapter 18 is the indictment of ' Babylon ' ; i.e. pagan Rome of the first century A.D. In 18. 12–13 we have the list of goods sold in the department stores, ending with ' horses and chariots and slaves and souls of men '. The merchants lament over the merchandise that no one will buy any more, and the ship-masters at the port of Ostia watch the smoke of the burning city (18. 11, 15, 17–19). Yet while a civilization perishes (18. 22–3), there are heard voices singing Alleluia, and praising God for His righteous judgements (19. 1–4).

ISAIAH AND THE REMNANT

As Isaiah was sure that after the LORD had 'performed His whole work upon mount Zion and upon Jerusalem', His judgement would fall upon Assyria (10. 12), so he believed that His chastisement of Jerusalem would lead to salvation.

It shall come to pass that he that is left in Zion,
And he that remaineth in Jerusalem,
  Shall be called holy,
Even every one that is written among the living at Jerusalem:
When the LORD shall have washed away the filth of the daughters
    of Zion,
And shall have purged the blood of Jerusalem from the midst
    thereof,
  By the spirit of judgment,
  And by the spirit of burning (4. 3–4).

The tree would have to be cut down, without mercy; yet the stump would remain (6. 13); and from the stump a new living shoot would spring up:

There shall come forth a shoot out of the stock of Jesse,
And a branch out of his roots shall bear fruit (11. 1).

'A remnant shall return' (*Shear-yashub*). He gave that name to his son (7. 3), in order to proclaim to all the doctrine of the Remnant. The faithful Remnant, purified through suffering, would no longer follow a policy of appeasement, but would put its trust in the Holy One of Israel (10. 20–1).

A nucleus of that Remnant was already discernible in the band of disciples which he gathered round him, disciples whom he believed God had given him, that through them He might work out His gracious purpose:

Behold, I and the children whom God hath given me,
Are for signs and wonders in Israel,
From the LORD of Hosts, which dwelleth in Mount Zion (8. 18).

The conception of a faithful Remnant had already appeared in the story of Elijah, who was told that he was not alone, as he thought, in his witness to the LORD and His truth (1 Kings 19. 10, 14):

I have been very jealous for the LORD, the God of Hosts; for the children of Israel have forsaken thy covenant, thrown down thine altars, and slain thy prophets with the sword: and I, even I only, am left, and they seek my life, to take it away;

but that there were seven thousand in Israel who had not bowed the knee to Baal (verse 18).

It had also been presented in pictorial form in the story of the Flood, which seems to be derived from ancient mythical sources, but which was told in Israel as a drama of a universal judgement of God upon the whole sinful race of men. This warning of a universal judgement was also given by the prophet Zephaniah, some seventy years later than Isaiah:

I will utterly consume all things from off the face of the ground,
   Saith the LORD.
  I will consume man and beast;
  I will consume the fowls of the heaven,
  And the fishes of the sea,
  And the stumbling-blocks with the wicked;
And I will cut off man from off the face of the ground,
   Saith the LORD. (Zeph. 1. 2–3.)

73

In the story of the Flood, Noah's Ark, riding on the waters, stands for the Remnant.

When at last Jerusalem was destroyed, there was a faithful Remnant which passed through the waters of judgement, and in which God's Purpose of salvation was carried on. Always after that there was a faithful Remnant, of those who were Israelites indeed. The idea, though not the name, comes again in the Son of Man prophecy of Dan. 7 (see pp. 136–7 below). When the Son of God hung on the Cross, the faithful Remnant existed in His person. St. Paul speaks of the Christians who believed in the Messiah though Israel as a whole had rejected Him, as ' a Remnant according to the election of grace ' (Rom. 11. 5) like the seven thousand who were found faithful in the time of Elijah (verses 2–4).

God's salvation always brings with it judgement. But in the midst of judgement there is always the Remnant, through which God's universal Purpose goes forward.

DEUTERONOMY AND JOSIAH'S REFORM

The prophets speak to a large extent (if the phrase may be allowed) in negative terms, convicting Israel of sin, throwing on contemporary life the light of God's truth which shows up the evil there. But there is another book, written about the same time, which sets out positively and constructively the pattern of what Israel's life should be ; this is the Book of Deuteronomy, which according to the generally accepted view is that Book of the Law which was found in the Temple by Hilkiah, as is related in 2 Kings 22. 8, and was put into practice in the Covenant made by King Josiah (23. 1–24). The date of this was 621 B.C. In spite of certain difficulties which remain only partly solved, this identification holds the field, and we can confidently say that the Book that Josiah had in his hands consisted of at least Deut. 12–26, though (as seems certain) additions were being made to the book for twenty or more years after.

In Deuteronomy the three main subjects of the prophetic preaching reappear somewhat as follows:

(1) The prophets had condemned the unreal worship of the LORD God. In Deuteronomy we get, up to chapter 11, splendid homilies about the faith of Israel, resting on the LORD's own act and the initiative which He took in redeeming Israel out of Egypt, not because of any merits on Israel's part, but solely because of His love (7. 7–8). We get the great *Shema*:

> Hear, O Israel, the LORD our God is one LORD; and thou shalt love the LORD thy God with all thy heart and with all thy soul and with all thy strength. And these words which I command thee this day shall be upon thine heart; and thou shalt teach them diligently unto thy children . . . (6. 4–7).

On Israel's loyalty to this faith and the spiritual service of the LORD which it demands, all its well-being and prosperity depends; disloyalty will as certainly bring judgement and punishment. Israel must remember God's dealing with it in the past: 'remember, remember . . .' (5. 15; 7. 18; 8. 2, 18; 9. 7, 27 &c.).

(2) The formal worship of the LORD, with dignity and splendour, was provided for by the centralization of all sacrifice in the great Temple at Jerusalem, and the destruction of all the country shrines which had originally been dedicated to Baal. This was ordered in Deut. 12. 1–7, 13–14, and carried out by Josiah (2 Kings 23. 4–15); it was however not a wholly new thing, for Hezekiah, 100 years before, had done something along these lines (2 Kings 18. 4). The intention was to cut off at the root the whole of the Canaanite nature-religion, that henceforth the religion of Israel might

be kept pure from pagan contamination. The commandment of Deut. 7. 2–3 that the Canaanites should be exterminated and that there should be no intermarriage with them, was of course wholly impracticable in the days of Josiah, for the intermarriage had taken place centuries before: indeed this commandment seems to be really an expression of regret, as if to say 'We ought to have exterminated the Canaanites when we entered Canaan, for then we should not have fallen away from the LORD into the worship of the Baalim.' But the commandment in 7. 5 to destroy the shrines could be and was put into practice. There was also this to it, that by this time the great agricultural festivals, which had originally been Baal-festivals, were now celebrated in honour of Yahweh, as is ordered in chapter 16. There was the Passover, the memorial of the deliverance from Egypt (16. 1–2), with the agricultural feast of Unleavened Bread (16. 3–4); then the Feast of Weeks, at the completion of the wheatharvest (16. 9–12); and the Feast of Tabernacles, the great annual festival in the autumn (16. 13–16).

It was true indeed that, just as no formal covenant or ordinance could guard against the unreal worship of the LORD God, so no prohibition of pagan practices could wholly stamp them out; and we find in Jer. 44. 17–19, 25, that incense was still being burned to the Queen of Heaven (Astarte) forty years later, after the Fall of Jerusalem: it had stopped in 621 B.C., and then had started again (44. 18). Yet it was a great thing indeed that the repudiation of idolatrous worship was now embodied in a covenant, solemnly entered on by king and people, and preserved in permanent form in a written book (2 Kings 23. 2–3). Indeed, this Book of Deuteronomy had now been accepted by Israel as authoritative and binding; in other words, it had become Scripture.

We are so used to having a Bible that it is easy to forget that there was once a time when no Bible existed, and, more than that, when the idea which the word 'Bible' signifies had not been thought of. There were of course in 621 B.C. many writings in existence which are now part of the Bible, but they were not solemnly authorized or treated as 'canonical'. But when Deuteronomy was accepted by king and people as the Book of the Covenant, the Book that contained God's commandments and that expressed Israel's faith, Israel had begun to have a Bible.

(3) The prophets had denounced social unrighteousness. Deuteronomy shows throughout how deep an impression their teaching had made. The regulations in chapters 12–26 are like a blue-print of the national life; the king is told what his duty is, and that he is to read in the book of the Law every day, 'that his heart be not lifted up above his brethren' (17. 14–20); judges must not pervert justice, nor take bribes (16. 18–20). There is a multitude of detailed regulations, largely taken from earlier codes, in chapters 19–26. But there is also an inculcation of generosity and kindliness, going beyond the written rule, as in 15. 7–11, about loans (22. 1–3), about lost property. The Book represents a determined effort to see the whole national life as under the rule of the LORD; and the making of Josiah's Covenant was the acceptance by the nation of Him as its King.

DID THE PROPHETIC TEACHING SUCCEED?

Was it really so? Was Israel really a 'converted nation', fit to be called the People of Yahweh? A wonderful Passover-festival was kept that year (2 Kings 23. 21–2). But Jeremiah, whose ministry had begun shortly before this, was bitterly disappointed. The national repentance had been skin-deep:

The sin of Judah is written with a pen of iron,
    And with the point of a diamond:
It is graven upon the table of their heart,
    And upon the horns of their altars,
While their children remember their altars and their Asherim
    By the green trees upon the high hills. (Jer. 17. 1–2.)

In 34. 18 he refers to the ceremony of the making of the
Covenant, when all the people passed between the halves of
a divided calf, and quoting (in verse 14) the law of Deut.
15. 12 about the release of Hebrew slaves, says that after
accepting this rule the masters had later gone back on it
(verses 9–11, 15–16). All through his ministry he was
seeing instance after instance of faithlessness, rebelliousness,
perversity, and relapse into idol-worship.

They were not a converted nation. From the human
point of view, the conflict of the faith of Yahweh with the
nature-religions and the sin in the heart of man had not
ended in anything that could really be called victory. As we
shall see in the next chapter, Jeremiah and Ezekiel laboured
to convince the people that the Fall of Jerusalem was a
deserved punishment.

But that is not to say that God's Purpose had failed.
His Purpose, as we shall see, was to go forward in spite of
and even by means of human failure. The decisive point
was, that in spite of all human shortcoming, His flag had
nevertheless been hoisted over the national life in the making
of the Deuteronomic Covenant. The Baal-shrines had
disappeared from Israel for ever. The principle of the one
sanctuary and the one altar, as the visible centre of unity for
God's People, had been asserted. There was the Book
of the Covenant, appealing back to the redemption from
Egypt as the ground of the nation's existence, and claiming
for Him the whole life of the People. A flag had been

hoisted which was never after to come down; it is still flying.

George Adam Smith, *The Book of the Twelve Prophets*, Vol. I. Hodder & Stoughton.

—— *The Book of Isaiah*, Vol. I. Hodder & Stoughton.

The Clarendon Bible, Vol. III : *The Decline and Fall of the Hebrew Kingdoms*, by T. H. Robinson. Oxford University Press, 1924.

Brilliant sketches of Amos, Hosea and Isaiah in :

W. A. L. Elmslie, *How came our Faith*. Cambridge University Press, 1948. (Chs. XII, XIII and XIV respectively.)

The ideal edition of the Prophets for the ordinary reader (cf. p. 64) :

F. H. Woods and F. E. Powell, *The Hebrew Prophets*, in 4 volumes. Oxford University Press, 1909–17.

CHAPTER VII

'Chastened and not killed'

JEREMIAH, EZEKIEL, SECOND ISAIAH

THE northern kingdom had perished in 721 B.C. The southern kingdom lasted for 135 years longer, when it too perished with the Fall of Jerusalem in 586 B.C. We cannot exaggerate the completeness of the disaster, when the whole fabric of the political, economic, and social life of the nation was destroyed, all the local traditions brought to an end, the city sacked, the Temple burnt with fire, the people (all but a few, mostly of the lowest class) deported to Meso-potamia. The intention of the conquerors was that the distinctive life of the free peoples should disappear, and the survivors from among them be merged in the Babylonian proletariat. That this did not happen in the case of Judah was an extraordinary thing, indeed altogether inexplicable apart from that which distinguished this nation from all others, namely its faith in Yahweh.

All the nations had their gods; and when one after another they were destroyed by militaristic Assyria, the conqueror could ask which of these gods had been able to deliver his people: ' where are the gods of Hamath and Arpad? where are the gods of Sepharvaim, of Hena, and Ivvah?' All these gods had been overpowered. Yahweh had been unable to save Samaria: it was vain to think that Jerusalem would escape (2 Kings 18. 33–6). Such was the argument of Rab-Shakeh to the people of Jerusalem in 701 B.C. In the next chapter we are told how King Hezekiah saw it. He prays to Yahweh, confesses Him to be God over all nations and kingdoms, being the creator of heaven and earth ; says that of course the nations have been destroyed and their gods thrown into the fire, 'for they were no gods, but the work of men's hands, wood and stone'; and prays that Yahweh will vindicate His honour by delivering Jerusalem (19. 15–19).

The prayer was heard, for the time being. But when the Day of Jerusalem came, there was still the faith that Yahweh was no mere personification of the genius of His nation, as the other tribal gods were, but was different. Of course His people were continually tempted, as we are still, to allow their religion to drop back on to a pagan level, and treat the Lord God as if He existed simply for the sake of the well-being and security of Israel. But Yahweh was different from the other gods. He was not (as it were) of one kin with Israel, their 'father': He had freely chosen them to be His people, and made His Covenant with them, and therefore had freedom of action with regard to them.

And when the blow fell, there was no denying the fact that since the days of Amos, 180 years before, a succession of prophets had said that He would chastise His People in just this way because of their sin. These prophecies had been most terribly verified by the event. There was, then, nothing for them to do but accept the fact, and confess that they had sinned. When they had done this difficult thing, the next point that became clear was that, if Yahweh had been chastising them, that proved that He cared about them, and had a purpose for them which He had yet to complete. He who had smitten was able to save. Thus it comes about that in the time of the Exile a series of Messianic prophecies appeared, of a fulness and richness hitherto unknown.

THEY WERE DEFEATED

But we must go back over the history. There were two Deportations, in 597 and 586. In 597 the king surrendered, and the Babylonians removed from the temple most of what was of value, and 10,000 captives, including the king and his chief men, and the fighting men and the craftsmen and artisans (2 Kings 24. 10–17). Among these was the prophet Ezekiel (Ezek. 1. 2). The difference between those who went and those who stayed seemed to Jeremiah like the difference between ' good figs, and figs that could not be eaten, they were so bad ' (Jer. 24).

The temptation now was to say, ' It is going to be all right. Yahweh delivered His people before in the time of King Hezekiah, and He will do so again. Within two years the exiles will be back home again, with the vessels belonging to the temple ; thus saith the LORD.' Exactly this was said by the prophet Hananiah, in Yahweh's name (Jer. 28. 1–4) ; and then he took a yoke which Jeremiah was wearing over his shoulders, as a token of the servitude which Yahweh was imposing on Judah and the surrounding nations (cf. 27. 2), and broke the yoke before the people, saying, ' Thus saith Yahweh, Even so will I break the yoke of Nebuchadnezzar King of Babylon ' (28. 5–11). Hananiah had won the first round. Jeremiah, however, tells us that the word of Yahweh came to him, that he must replace the wooden yoke with a yoke of iron, and explain what this meant, and say to Hananiah that he was making the people to trust in a lie, and would die within the year because he had spoken rebellion against Yahweh ; and that Hananiah died in the seventh month (28. 12–17).

Ezekiel was saying much the same to the exiles in Babylon. They must not listen to the plausible prophets ' who seduce

my people, saying Peace, where there is no peace' (13. 1–10).
Those prophets are building a wall with untempered mortar,
and the wall is going to come crashing down (13. 10–16).
Jerusalem is going to fall; it must fall, because of the sins
of the people (see chapter 8, where the prophet is taken in a
trance to Jerusalem, and sees the abominations being practised there; chapters 9, 10 and 11 continue with a 'mystical'
description of the fall of the city). He uses one means
after another to bring home to the exiles that it will be so
and must be so; they themselves must confess their sin
(chapter 18), and the sin of rebellion against the LORD which
has been shown in each period of the nation's history from
the beginning (20. 1–44).

The prophet's word was indeed to be vindicated by the
event; but the cost of it to Ezekiel himself can be guessed
from what he tells us of his own wife's death. He was told
by the LORD that he was to make no sign of mourning,
though his heart was breaking with grief:

The word of the LORD came unto me, saying,
   ' Son of man, behold, I take away from thee the desire of thine
      eyes with a stroke :
   Yet neither shalt thou mourn nor weep,
   Neither let thy tears run down.
   Sigh, but not aloud;
   Make no mourning for the dead . . .'
So I spake unto the people in the morning; and at even my wife
died : and I did in the morning as I was commanded (24. 15–18).

When the people asked what could be the reason for this
extraordinary behaviour, he told them that it would be so
with them when the City fell; it would be so utterly crushing
a blow that it would leave them speechless, and unable even
to weep :

Thus saith the Lord GOD:
  Behold, I will profane my sanctuary,
      The pride of your power,
      The desire of your eyes,
      And that which your soul pitieth:
      And your sons and your daughters whom ye have left
        behind shall fall by the sword.
  And ye shall do as I have done: . . .
      Ye shall not mourn nor weep;
      But ye shall pine away in your iniquities,
      And moan one toward another.
  Thus shall Ezekiel be to you a sign;
  According to all that he hath done shall ye do:
  When this cometh, then shall ye know that I am the Lord
      GOD (24. 21–4).

In Ezek. 37 we have the vision of the Valley of the Dry
Bones: the valley was like the site of a battlefield. Could
those bones live? He was told to prophesy, and bid spirit,
wind, breath (these are all one word in Hebrew) to enter
into those slain that they might live. He prophesied, and
there was a weird movement of bones coming together, and
flesh and sinews covering the bones, so that they had the
semblance of real men; but there was no life in them
(37. 1–8). Such, Ezekiel thought, were the Israelites to
whom he prophesied. They had at the catastrophe been
a mob of survivors, a social structure completely broken
up into isolated individuals. As he prophesied, they seemed
to be coming together into something which bore some
remote likeness to what the People of God should be: but
there was no life there, they were quite dead. They were
saying, ' Our bones are dried up, our hope is lost, we are
clean cut off ' (37. 11). But he is told that he must go on
prophesying, till at last they ' stand on their feet, an exceeding
great army '.

Meanwhile Jeremiah had written to the exiles of the First
Deportation a famous letter (Jer. 29. 1–3) in which he told
them to settle down in Babylonia, build houses, and seek
the peace of the city whither they were carried away captive;
for there would be no speedy return; it would not be for
seventy years (4–10). But Yahweh had the whole matter
in hand (verse 11), and they must pray to Him in Babylon
(12): 'and ye shall seek me and find me, when ye shall
seek for me with all your heart' (13). But the immediate
prospect for Jerusalem was ruin (16–19).

Jer. 29. 13, which has just been quoted, is almost word for
word the same as Deut. 4. 29. There it is said (Deut. 4. 25–6)
that if the people sin and corrupt themselves, they shall perish
out of the land of Canaan, and shall be scattered in foreign
lands (27), where they will be subject to the gods of the land
who are no-gods (28). But if from thence they seek Yahweh
their God, they shall find Him, if they seek with all their
heart and all their soul (29), for He will not fail them (30, 31).
Then comes the passage quoted at length on p. 48 above,
where it is said that the revelation of Yahweh in His mighty
works wrought out in history is absolutely unique, and there
is nothing like it among all the religions of the nations (32–5).
For ' Yahweh, he is God, in heaven above and earth beneath;
there is none else ' (verse 39).

Such were the thoughts about God to which the Israelites
began to come, when in the midst of their utterly crushing
affliction they called upon the God in whom they had believed
(more or less) from childhood. Yet they had seen His temple
desecrated and burned with fire, the city walls broken down
and the city ruined; they had seen most of their kinsfolk
and friends suffer violent death or things worse than death,
or perish by famine. (All this is vividly pictured in Lam. 2.
15–22.) It had been the hour of Israel's passion; and a

terrible tribulation it had been. But now out of the midst of suffering came hope; a hope based on a faith that faced all the facts and claimed no exemption: faith that Yahweh the God of Israel was the Lord of the whole earth and the ruler of history; faith that in His dealings with Israel He had been righteous; and a hope that looked towards the future accomplishment of His purpose in history.

The hope of the final accomplishment of God's purpose in history is what we call the Messianic Hope, which found its greatest expression in this period, in the prophets Jeremiah, Ezekiel and Second Isaiah. We will set this out in the next chapter: we must first say a little more about the life of Israel in exile.

ISRAEL IN EXILE

We have no historical narrative of this period. But we can infer a great deal from the facts which we know:

(1) The faithful Israelites did not become absorbed in the Mesopotamian proletariat, but held together as a believing and worshipping community. In Ezekiel's day, as we have seen, they were at least holding together. A generation later, Second Isaiah could address to them glowing words of encouragement; while at the end of the next century (about 400 B.C.), Ezra led a return of Jews to Jerusalem, strong in numbers and strong in faith, to make a new start in the restored temple. It follows from this that the exiles had found means to meet together and worship God and be instructed in the Faith, and grow together into a believing community.

(2) The writings containing their old traditions were preserved by these Jews of the Exile: all those books which we have been studying; most of Genesis, some of Exodus and Numbers, Deuteronomy; and the books from Joshua to

Kings in an unfinished state, the books of the pre-exilic prophets, and a number of psalms.   They preserved these writings not for antiquarian purposes, but because their whole
faith rested on Yahweh's action in history, and these were the
records of His dealings with Abraham, Isaac, and Jacob, and
above all of the Deliverance from Egypt and the Covenant;
and after that, of the story of their life in Canaan and the sin
against Yahweh for which they were now suffering the
punishment of exile.   Every Israelite needed to know these
things : therefore he needed to be told, indeed to be systema-
tically instructed in what his membership in Israel involved,
as a faith to believe and a duty to do.

(3) In present-day Judaism there exists the Synagogue, and
its purpose is precisely what was said in the last sentence : to
instruct and exercise the Jew in his faith and duty.   In New
Testament days multitudes of Synagogues were to be found,
wherever there were Jews.   How early they began, we do not
know.   But there is a description in Neh. 8 of an open-air
meeting which recalls several features of the Synagogue :
Ezra reads from the Book of the Law, standing in a pulpit
of wood (8. 1–4) ; the people stand up and answer " Amen "
(6) ; the Levites explain the meaning of what has been
read (7–8).

In the old days in Canaan, the people continually met at
the Temple and elsewhere.   But neither there, nor anywhere
else in antiquity, were buildings constructed to house a congregation.   An ancient sanctuary was built to house the
image of the god, or (in the case of Solomon's temple) the
sacred Ark, and provide strong-rooms for the offerings ; the
people were never allowed inside, but stood round the altar
in the open air.   But in Babylonia there was nowhere for
them to meet, except in some house ; and we hear of them
meeting in Ezekiel's house (Ezek. 8. 1 ; 14. 1 ; 20. 1).   For

serious religious instruction a house was necessary; and whenever it was that such houses began to be built, then for the first time in history buildings were being built to hold a congregation. And our churches are still synagogues—with pulpit, benches, and a lectern for the Book, with the addition of a receptacle for baptismal water, the Table of the Lord's Supper, and a chair for a successor of the apostles : further, the items of the synagogue service—prayer and praise, scripture readings and exposition of scripture—reappear in the ante-communion and the sermon, or in Mattins or Evensong with sermon, while the action at the Lord's Table which begins with the Offertory and goes on to the Consecration and Communion, is that which has taken the place of the Temple sacrifices.

The inference seems inevitable, that in principle the synagogue began in the early days of the Exile, and that the reading of the Law and the other books in the Synagogue played an important part in the formation of the Canon of the Old Testament. In exile, they had Deuteronomy; it needed to be read and expounded. To the exhortations of Deuteronomy, which centred in the story of God's redemptive action in the Exodus, were added the narratives of the Exodus : to the Laws in Deuteronomy, the other laws which existed. Here is the nucleus of the Pentateuch ; the nucleus consists of the story of God's mighty acts, and the commandments which man was set to keep.

In the later Synagogue there was a Lesson also from the prophets (Acts 13. 15). In the Hebrew Bible the 'earlier Prophets' are the historical books from Joshua to Kings, and the 'later prophets' are Isaiah, Jeremiah, Ezekiel, and 'the twelve' (minor prophets). The whole Bible is referred to in Luke 24. 44 as 'the law, the prophets and the psalms'. This third division is called in the Hebrew Bible the Kethubim

or ' Writings '.   It was natural that the psalms used in worship should be included in the Scripture, together with the
other writings of a more miscellaneous character, which make
up the rest of the Old Testament.

The religious life of Israel as it grew up during and after
the Exile developed a strong and imposing structure.   Truly
those who built it up after the great catastrophe were men of
great faith.   Taking their instructions from Jeremiah's great
letter, they called upon Yahweh (to all outward appearance,
the presiding genius of an insignificant and defeated nation),
believing that He was the Lord of the whole world and the
lord of history ; and that the Babylonian gods (the presiding
genii of the greatest civilization then existing) were no-gods
and vanity.   We have now reached the historical situation in
which Genesis 1 was written, and also the prophecies of
Second Isaiah which we placed side by side with them.   The
reader will perhaps like to refer back to chapter II of this book.
To believe in God is always an act of faith.   In those men
and at that time it was heroic faith.

The Jew now saw his nation as entrusted with this faith :
we shall see in the next chapter how his greatest teachers
taught him that this faith was held in trust for people of all
nations.   In this connexion it is of interest to refer to another
chapter which gives the outlook of P (the ' priestly writer '),
and of the Jews in Babylon, on the civilization around them :
Gen. 9. 1–17, especially 8–17, about the Covenant of Noah
between God and ' all flesh ' (verses 11, 15, 16, 17) ; for Noah
is the ancestor of all mankind.   This chapter has played a
large part in Jewish thought since, and rightly.   It describes
the life of manhood in general, his dominion over the animals,
and right to use them for food (verses 1–3) : the sacredness
of human life, and the death penalty for murder (because man
is made in God's image, verse 6 : cf. 1. 26) ; and the command

to be fruitful and multiply (9. 1, 7). Of God's covenant
with all flesh, ' that the waters shall no more become a flood to
destroy all flesh ', the rainbow is the sign (14-15).

THE SERVANT OF THE LORD

Israel was the chosen people of Yahweh : and the vocation
of Israel, both in regard to its service of Him and its duty to
the heathen population around, is set out in four poems which
form the greatest treasure, perhaps, in the whole Old Testament : the Poems of the Servant of the LORD in Isa. 42. 1-4;
49. 1-6; 50. 4-9; 52. 13 - 53. 12. But though the poems
can be thus separated off, they also belong to their context
in the prophecy; the first two poems are both expanded in
the chapters to which they belong. It is a subject of perennial
discussion who the Servant is—some person (a saint like
Jeremiah)—or the actual Israel—or Israel as God means it to
be—or a Person who shall some day appear : but the best
expositors seem to say that, at least as regards the Last of
the Poems, the Servant is One who is yet to come, for His
work is described as an accepted sacrifice (53. 10), as redemptive suffering by which sin is overcome and taken away
(53. 11-12).

The four Poems are quoted very much in the New Testament. But let us see them in the light of their original occa-
sion. The Israelites had been through a period of fearful,
crushing, desolating suffering; and suffering is not rendered
less terrible when relatively small numbers are involved.
They were coming, through suffering, to a firm, victorious
faith. The suffering, then, had a meaning; all suffering
could have a meaning, and in suffering patiently borne according to God's will there was victory over sin.

Such are the meditations of this greatest of Israel's saints
and poets. First, there is the picture of the true Servant of

the LORD, the Israelite indeed, rendering to God spiritual service according to His will; not by ways of self-advertisement, but by patient ministry to ' the bruised reed ', he is to grow in grace and not fail nor be discouraged, till his witness has been borne to the Gentiles also, and they have listened (42. 1–4) :

Behold my Servant, whom I uphold;
My chosen, in whom my soul delighteth :
I have put my Spirit upon him;
He shall bring forth judgment to the Gentiles.
He shall not cry, nor lift up, nor cause his voice to be heard in the
    street.
A bruised reed shall he not break,
And the smoking flax shall he not quench :
He shall bring forth judgment in truth.
He shall not fail nor be discouraged,
Till he hath set judgment in the earth,
And the isles shall wait for his law. (42. 1–4.)

In the second poem, the Servant himself speaks; he is conscious of a vocation from his birth, and that he is called to be an instrument in God's hand, sharp and effective, to be used for God's glory. Tempted to discouragement, when his witness seems to be all in vain, he leaves all to God; and then he learns that his mission, his vocation for which he was called from his birth, is not only to minister to the chosen people, and gather them together as the People of the LORD, but also to be a light to the Gentiles in all parts of the earth :

Listen, O isles, unto me;
And hearken, ye peoples, from far :
The LORD hath called me from the womb;
From the bowels of my mother hath he made mention of my name :

And he hath made my mouth like a sharp sword,
In the shadow of his hand hath he hid me;
And he hath made me a polished shaft,
In his quiver hath he kept me close:
And he said to me, 'Thou art my Servant,
   Israel, in whom I will be glorified.'

But I said, 'I have laboured in vain,
I have spent my strength for nought and vanity:
Yet surely my judgment is with the LORD,
   And my recompense with my God.'
And now saith the LORD that formed me from the womb to be his
     Servant,
   To bring Jacob again to him,
   And that Israel be gathered unto him:
   (For I am honourable in the eyes of the LORD,
   And my God is become my strength:)
Yea, he saith,
  'It is too light a thing that thou shouldest be my Servant
    To raise up the tribes of Jacob,
    And to restore the preserved of Israel:
  I will also give thee for a light to the Gentiles,
  That thou mayest be my salvation unto the end of the earth.'
    (49. 1–6.)

In the third poem, the Servant again speaks. It is for him
to be a disciple, and to wait morning by morning for the
LORD's word, with a sensitive ear; he has followed this way
obediently, in spite of cruel persecution which he has patiently
endured, trusting in God's vindication of His Servant:

The Lord GOD hath given me the tongue of them that are taught
That I should know how to sustain with words him that is weary:
  He wakeneth morning by morning,
  He wakeneth mine ear to hear as they that are taught.

The Lord GOD hath opened mine ear,
  And I was not rebellious,
  Neither turned away backward.
I gave my back to the smiters,
  And my cheeks to them that plucked off the hair:
I hid not my face from shame and spitting.

For the Lord GOD will help me;
Therefore have I not been confounded:
Therefore have I set my face like a flint,
And I know that I shall not be ashamed.

  He is near that justifieth me;
  Who will contend with me?
    Let us stand up together;
  Who is mine adversary?
    Let him come near to me.

Behold, the Lord GOD will help me:
  Who is he that shall condemn me?
Behold, they all shall wax old as a garment;
  The moth shall eat them up. (50. 4–9.)

In the fourth poem, the Servant is not the speaker, but
others speak about Him—indeed they can do no else than
speak about Him. It consists of five stanzas, in each of
which the first phrase gives the theme of the stanza, and is
here printed in italics. In eight places the marginal rendering
is used.

In the first stanza God speaks: His Servant (taken as
known from the other poems) shall prosper (i.e. prevail, as
one who 'deals wisely' and, as we say, makes good); He
shall be vindicated by God, though many have been shocked
at Him, and misunderstood His suffering (52. 12–15):

Behold, my Servant shall prosper,
He shall be exalted and lifted up, and shall be very high.
Like as many were astonied at thee
  (His visage was so marred from that of man,
  And his form from that of the sons of men),
So shall he startle many nations;
Kings shall shut their mouths at him:
For that which had not been told them shall they see;
And that which they had not heard shall they understand.

In the second, the people speak (perhaps Gentiles, perhaps Israelites; but it is best to leave it indefinite, as 'we'). 'Who of us', they say, 'believed what we were told? None of us. We saw the LORD's Servant suffer, and we despised Him' (53. 1–3):

Who hath believed that which we heard?
And to whom hath the arm of the LORD been revealed?
For he grew up before him as a tender plant,
  And as a root out of a dry ground:
He hath no form nor comeliness;
  And when we see him,
There is no beauty that we should desire him.
He was despised and rejected of men;
A man of sorrows, and acquainted with sickness:
And as one from whom men hide their face
  He was despised, and we esteemed him not.

In the third, the people again speak: 'Now we understand; it was the sicknesses and sorrows due to us that He was bearing; He was suffering for us. It was we who had offended, going astray like sheep: He bore it all' (4–6):

Surely he hath borne our sicknesses, and carried our sorrows:
Yet we did esteem him stricken, smitten of God, and afflicted.
But he was wounded for our transgressions,

He was bruised for our iniquities:
The chastisement of our peace was upon him;
And with his stripes we are healed.
All we like sheep have gone astray;
We have turned every one to his own way;
And the LORD hath laid on him the iniquity of us all.

In the fourth, the prophet interprets the meaning further. The LORD's Servant, patiently enduring cruelty practised on Him, and suffering condemnation through miscarriage of justice, died a martyr's death (7–9).

He was oppressed,
Yet he humbled himself and opened not his mouth;
  As a lamb that is led to the slaughter,
  And as a sheep that before her shearers is dumb;
Yea, he opened not his mouth.
By oppression and judgment he was taken away;
And as for his generation, who among them considered
  That he was cut off out of the land of the living?
For the transgression of my people was he stricken.
And they made his grave with the wicked,
  And with the rich in his death;
Although he had done no violence,
Neither was any deceit in his mouth.

In the fifth, the prophet speaks in God's Name, till in verses 11 and 12 it is God Himself speaking: 'In all this God's own work of salvation is seen: the Servant's martyrdom is an accepted sacrifice, and the end shall be blessing and peace. His work accomplished, His soul shall be satisfied, when He sees how souls have been saved from the power of evil. The Servant of the LORD is a great conqueror, through giving His life up to death, being counted as a wrong-doer, and in all this bearing the sin of others and praying for them.'

Yet it pleased the LORD *to bruise him;*
He hath made him sick:
  When thou shalt make his soul a guilt-offering,
He shall see his seed,
He shall prolong his days,
And the pleasure of the LORD shall prosper in his hand.
' He shall see of the travail of his soul, and shall be satisfied:
By his knowledge shall my righteous Servant justify many:
  And he shall bear their iniquities.
Therefore will I divide him a portion with the great,
And he shall divide the spoil with the strong;
Because he poured out his soul unto death,
And was numbered with the transgressors:
Yet he bare the sin of many,
And made intercession for the transgressors.'

Such would be the Divine way of salvation. So should God's victory be won.

Israel in Exile:

A. G. Hebert, *The Authority of the Old Testament.* Faber, 1947. (Ch. V.)

The Servant-Poems:

George Adam Smith, *The Book of Isaiah.* Hodder & Stoughton. (Vol. II, pp. 236–374.)

The arrangement of the Servant-songs in lines is copied from Woods and Powell, *The Hebrew Prophets,* Vol. III.

CHAPTER VIII

' *Behold, thy King cometh unto thee* '

THE MESSIANIC PROPHECIES

WE can think, then, of the remnant of Israel in exile, trying to reckon it all up, and see what it all meant : the desolating catastrophe, and the loss of everything in the world that they had held dear, and their present wretched life in an alien land ; and a message was coming through that there was a meaning in it. There was a letter, and some other prophecies, from Jeremiah in far-away Palestine ; and among them was a hard-faced man with a strange tenderness in him, a man given to queer ecstasies and strange trances, but who spoke with such conviction that they could not help but listen :

And as for thee, son of man, the children of thy people talk of thee by the walls and in the doors of the houses, and speak one to another, every one to his brother, saying, ' Come, I pray you, and hear the word that cometh forth from the LORD.'

And they come unto thee as the people cometh,

And they sit before thee as my people,

And they hear thy words,

But do them not :

For with their mouth they show much love,

But their heart goeth after their gain.

And lo, thou art unto them as a very lovely song of one that hath a pleasant voice,

And can play well on an instrument :

For they hear thy words,

But do them not.

And when this cometh to pass, (behold, it cometh) then shall they know that a prophet hath been among them (Ezek. 33. 30–3).

Ezekiel refers in the last sentence, no doubt, to the impending news of the final ruin of Jerusalem, though the news is said to have come through in verse 21 of the same chapter; the prophecies are not necessarily in strict chronological order.

It was a hard, hard message that he had to give. They had sinned against their God, and this terrible calamity had come from Him: it was His doing, and He was punishing them for their sin. Yet it made sense. It was what some of the prophets whom they had dreaded and disliked had been saying for a long time before. But their consciences told them that it was true. And it held within it a spring of wonderful hope; for if it were true, it meant that Yahweh, their God, with whom all their previous life had been bound up, was not defeated, had not been overpowered in the disaster that had fallen on Jerusalem, and that He was not indifferent to them now, but still cared for them, and still had a purpose for them.

The message, as it came through and slowly became clear to them, was that Yahweh had a great and glorious Purpose in store, wonderful beyond words. He who (as they had always believed) had in the distant past delivered their fathers from Egypt in the Exodus, would when His time had come deliver them again in *another and a more glorious Exodus*, and lead them back to Jerusalem in triumph; would make with them *a New Covenant*, and reconcile them to Himself as a truly converted Israel, *pouring out His Spirit* upon them, that they might truly be His people, and He their God, and forgiving them all their sin. And further, that when *He manifested His glory* in this new deliverance, *all the heathen around them would be brought in*, to share in this new knowledge of Him as the gracious and merciful God. The italicized

98

phrases give five points, which we shall use as headings for our exposition in this chapter.

It was a hope of a fresh series of divine acts in history, of a future Day when God would complete His Purpose for Israel; when the age of miracles would begin again, and things hitherto impossible become possible. We shall see when we come to the Fulfilment in Jesus Christ how it is chiefly to these prophecies that our Lord and His apostles appeal.

THE MESSIANIC KING

We must go back first, for a moment, to Amos and the first Isaiah, before we come to the Messianic prophecies of the Exile, in Jeremiah, Ezekiel, and Second Isaiah.

In Amos, as we saw on p. 65, we find that people were hopefully anticipating a 'Day of the LORD' which would bring peace, security, and blessedness, in a wonderful 'Golden Age.' Amos said that the 'Day of the LORD' would be 'darkness and not light'; when the LORD God came, He would come to judge them for their sins (Amos 5. 18, 22–3).

Isaiah took up the same dreadful message, but saw in it a future Salvation as well as Judgement. He saw a Day coming when all nations would seek the Law of Yahweh at Jerusalem (2. 2–4: this comes also in Mic. 4. 1–3: it is quoted on p. 100 below); when the penitent Remnant of Israel, purified by much suffering, would be fit to be called 'holy' (Isa. 4. 2–4: quoted on p. 72 above); when the Deliverer would be called *Immanuel*, 'God with us' (7. 14–15); would reign on the throne of David, as a King called by wonderful Names, and ruling in righteousness:

> For unto us a child is born,
> Unto us a son is given;
> And the government shall be upon his shoulder:

And his name shall be called
   Wonderful, Counsellor,
   Mighty God,
   Everlasting Father,
   Prince of Peace (9. 6);

as a king of David's line, filled with the Spirit of the LORD :

And there shall come forth a shoot out of the stock of Jesse,
And a branch out of his roots shall bear fruit :
And the Spirit of the LORD shall rest upon him,
   The Spirit of wisdom and understanding,
   The Spirit of counsel and might,
   The Spirit of knowledge and of the fear of the LORD ;
And his delight shall be in the fear of the LORD :
And he shall not judge after the sight of his eyes,
Neither reprove after the hearing of his ears
But with righteousness shall he judge the poor,
And reprove with equity for the meek of the earth . . . (11. 1–4).

In Isaiah's day Judah was ruled by the godly king Hezekiah ; and he saw the glorious Future as a day when a greater than Hezekiah would rule in a Jerusalem which had passed through a searching judgement and would truly be a ' City of Righteousness, a faithful city' (1. 26). Thus Isaiah's hopes of a glorious Future had their setting in the actual Jerusalem which he knew.

But the time was not yet. Isaiah, like so many after him, believed and expected that the Day of the LORD would appear very soon. As regards the time, both he and they were mistaken. As regards the outward shape of the deliverance —a king holding temporal power and ruling over Israel—he was also mistaken. There was to be a King, but a King who was to be crowned with thorns, and who was to bring a more radical and thorough Deliverance than any temporal ruler could effect. We shall study the nature of His kingship later (pp. 146–54 below). The sort of transformation of Isaiah's hope that would take place was to be indicated by the poems of the Servant of the Lord, and by the Messianic predictions of the prophets of the Exile. These naturally divide themselves up under five headings.

(1) THE SECOND EXODUS

Jeremiah, about the time of the catastrophe, was saying that there would be a new Deliverance, like the Exodus from Egypt. He says in 23. 5 that the King whom Isaiah promised would appear (for the 'righteous Branch' in 23. 5 is the same as the 'Shoot of the stock of Jesse', Isa. 11. 1), and then that the time will come when they will no longer invoke the Name of the LORD as of Him who brought Israel out of Egypt, but of Him as the Deliverer who will have brought Israel back from all the lands of the Exile.

Behold the days come, saith the LORD,
That I will raise unto David a righteous Branch,
And he shall reign as king and deal wisely,
And shall execute judgment and justice in the land.
In his days Judah shall be saved,
And Israel shall dwell safely:
And this is his name whereby he shall be called,
  'The LORD our Righteousness'.
Therefore, behold, the days come, saith the LORD,
That they shall no more say
  'As the LORD liveth,
  Which brought up the children of Israel
  Out of the land of Egypt';
But, 'As the LORD liveth,
  Which brought up and which led the seed of the house of Israel
  Out of the north country,
    And from all the countries whither I had driven them':
And they shall dwell in their own land. (Jer. 23. 5–8.)

We shall see, when we come to the New Testament, how we still speak of our Lord's Resurrection as a 'crossing of the Red Sea'; and that God has 'loosed from Pharoah's bitter yoke, Jacob's sons and daughters, Led them with unmoistened foot Through the Red Sea waters' (*Hymns Ancient and Modern* 133, *English Hymnal* 131). But we are concerned now with the prophets of the Exile.

Second Isaiah plainly has this New Exodus in mind, when in 40. 3 he speaks of 'preparing in the wilderness' or desert, 'a highway for our God'; and later on, of the Lord as making 'a way in the sea, and a path in the mighty waters', and bringing forth 'the chariot and the horse' which shall be overthrown, and then says, 'Remember ye not the former things' (the first Exodus) for 'behold I will do a new thing . . . I will even make a way in the wilderness, and rivers in the desert' (43. 16–19); and he refers in verse 20 to the bringing of the water out of the rock in the desert by Moses (Exod. 17. 2–7). This allusion comes again in Isa. 48. 21. The 'drying up of the sea' (Exod. 14) is alluded to again in Isa. 50. 2, 51. 10; and in 52. 12 he says 'Ye shall not go out in haste, neither shall ye go by flight' (as in the first Exodus); 'for the Lord will go before you' (as then in the Pillar of Cloud) 'and the God of Israel will be your rereward.'

(2) THE NEW COVENANT

Of old, the Lord had made His Covenant with Israel at Horeb, after bringing them out of Egypt. Jeremiah sees His future Purpose for Israel as a new Exodus followed by a new Covenant:

Behold, the days come, saith the Lord, that I will make a New Covenant with the house of Israel, and with the house of Judah : Not according to the Covenant that I made with their fathers in

the day that I took them by the hand to bring them out of the
and of Egypt;

Which my Covenant they brake, although I was an husband
unto them,
                          Saith the LORD.
But this is the Covenant that I will make with the house of Israel
          after those days, saith the LORD :
  I will put my law in their inward parts,
  And in their heart will I write it;
        And I will be their God,
  And they shall be my People ;
  And they shall teach no more every man his neighbour,
        And every man his brother,
        Saying, know the LORD :
  For they shall all know me,
  From the least of them unto the greatest of them,
                          Saith the LORD :
  For I will forgive their iniquity,
  And their sin will I remember no more.   (Jer. 31. 31–4.)

This prophecy is one of the landmarks in the history of the
People of God.   The New Covenant is to be characterized
by the Law of God being not a mere external rule, but written
in the heart; the knowledge of God is to be no more at
second-hand, learnt from some prophet or priest, but personal knowledge ; and there is to be full forgiveness of sins.
This prophecy has set the pattern of all Christian spirituality.

At the Last Supper, our LORD declared that this prophecy
was now fulfilled, through the Sacrifice of the Messiah :
'This cup is the New Covenant, in my blood' (1 Cor. 11.25);
and it was ' for the forgiveness of sins ' (Matt. 26. 28).

(3) THE GIFT OF THE SPIRIT OF THE LORD

First Isaiah (11. 2) had spoken of the six-fold gift of the
Spirit of Yahweh to the Messianic king : now we hear of the
Spirit to be poured out on the Messianic people.

The prophecy of Joel, quoted by St. Peter at Pentecos
(Acts 2. 17–21), promises that the Spirit of the LORD will be
given when the Day of the LORD comes with cosmic wonders
(2. 30–1), and the believing Remnant, of whom the first
Isaiah had spoken long before, should receive God's salvation
(verse 32) ; and the sign of the Spirit's coming would be that
all people would receive that same gift that was given to the
prophets : the old should dream dreams, and the young
should see visions (verses 28–9). Here, then, the Spirit is
to impart prophetic insight.

Ezekiel goes deeper, and sees the fruit of the Spirit to be
a truly converted heart, and a complete and entire obedience
to God's will, thus reversing the disobedience and rebelliousness for which He had punished His people in the great
catastrophe (Ezek. 36. 25–7) :

> I will sprinkle clean water upon you
> And ye shall be clean ;
> From all your filthiness, and from all your idols
> Will I cleanse you.
> A new heart also will I give you,
> And a new spirit will I put within you ;
> And I will take away the stony heart out of your flesh,
> And I will give you an heart of flesh.
> And I will put my Spirit within you,
> And cause you to walk in my statutes,
> And ye shall keep my judgments and do them.

The phrases are different from Jeremiah's prophecy of the
New Covenant ; but is not the essential meaning as good as
identical ? The Purpose of the LORD, which began when
He called Israel out of Egypt and made the Covenant at
Horeb, is to find its fulfilment in the entire acceptance by
Israel of its vocation, bringing to God not mere obedience
to an outward law, but the love of a wholly surrendered heart.

In the centuries that followed, before our Lord's coming, the Israelites were to be set to learn what this meant, and to be tempted to substitute the keeping of an outward law for the loving of God with all their heart and soul and mind. Our Lord, when He came, recalled them to the things that the prophets had said. The Gospel word ' repent ' means much more than merely being sorry for past misdeeds ; it means literally a ' change of attitude ' just such as Ezekiel depicts, in the change from the heart of stone to the heart of flesh, sensitive and responsive. And with our Lord it is no mere hope of something that God will do in the future, but a present challenge ; for with Him the age of miracles begins again, and this is what it demands.

(4) THE RETURN OF THE PRESENCE

Here we come to a thought closely connected with the New Exodus. When the LORD again takes action to deliver His people, He will be in their midst as at Mount Horeb, where the Covenant was made. There, the smoke of the volcano was ' as the smoke of a furnace ' (Exod. 19. 18). But the Presence is depicted also as being with the Israelites at the Crossing of the Red Sea, in the form of a Pillar of Cloud (Exod. 14. 24)—as though the pillar-like cloud of volcanic smoke were detached from the mountain and became movable ; for the Pillar of Cloud ' descended and stood at the door of the Tent ' or the ' Tabernacle ', when Moses went in and spoke with Him (Exod. 33. 9), and is mentioned in Num. 10. 33–4 in connexion with the Sacred Ark, as the symbol of the LORD'S presence with His people through the wilderness-period.

When the Ark was lost to the Philistines in the days of Eli, the baby that was born was called *Ichabod*, ' the Glory is departed from Israel ' (1 Sam. 4. 21) ; for this word ' Glory ' is constantly found to describe the Presence on the Sacred Ark. When the Ark had been recovered, and Solomon's Temple was dedicated, we read

And it came to pass, when the priests were gone out of the holy place, that the Cloud filled the house of the LORD, so that the priests could not stand to minister by reason of the Cloud ; for the Glory of the LORD filled the house of the LORD (1 Kings 8. 10, 11).

When Jerusalem was taken and the Temple burned with fire, Ezekiel tells us how the Presence departed. This came to him in a long trance-like experience (from Ezek. 8. 1 to 10. 25) in which he saw, first the idolatries being carried on in the Temple (chapter 8), then the slaughter at the fall of the city (chapter 9), then the vision of the Presence in the cherub chariot (chapter 10) which at 10. 19 is seen ' at the door of the east gate of the LORD's house ', and in 11. 22–3 is seen moving away, and resting on the Mount of Olives as It departs.

But It would come back. After Ezekiel has described the plan of the rebuilt city and Temple, he sees the Presence returning and entering the House by the east gate ;

And, behold, the Glory of the God of Israel came from the way of the east and his voice was like the sound of many waters ; and the earth shined with his Glory. . . . And the Glory of the LORD came into the house, by the way of the gate whose prospect is toward the east . . . and behold, the Glory of the LORD filled the house. And I heard one speaking unto me out of the house ; and a man stood by me. And he said unto me,
' Son of man, this is the place of my throne,
And the place of the soles of my feet,
Where I will dwell in the midst of the children of Israel for ever :
And the house of Israel shall no more defile my holy name.'
(Ezek. 43. 2, 4–7.)

And Ezekiel is permitted to make known to them what is to be the form of the house, and the ordinances connected with it, provided that they are truly penitent and are ' ashamed of all that they have done ' (verses 10–11).

So then, when the Day of the LORD came, He would return in visible presence to dwell in the midst of His penitent and forgiven people, as of old His presence had been with them in the Wilderness. It is this of which Second Isaiah was speaking, when he declared that the way of the LORD's coming was to be prepared in the wilderness (Isa. 40. 3), and every valley be exalted and every mountain and hill made low: for ' the Glory of the LORD shall be revealed, and all flesh shall see it together; for the mouth of the LORD hath spoken it ' (verse 5). Hence the cry which the watchman is to give is ' Behold your God ' (verse 9) : ' behold, the Lord GOD will come as a mighty one, and his arm shall rule for him ' and ' He shall feed his flock like a shepherd ', caring for the lambs and the mothers that give suck (verses 10, 11).

The prophet believed that a mighty divine action was imminent; and he called, as it seems, on the exiles to go to Jerusalem and await there the next act in the unfolding of God's purpose (Isa. 52. 11). The whole prophecy resounds with the certainty that this great Deliverance was coming; it would be connected with the coming of the Persian King Cyrus: ' Thus saith the LORD to his anointed, to Cyrus ' (45. 1). Here the word ' anointed ' is in Hebrew *Messiah*. The prophet does not, of course, mean that the heathen king is ' the Messiah ' in the later sense of the word; for it was not till four or five centuries later that the word ' Messiah ' came to be used in the technical sense which it bears in the gospels, where Peter hails Jesus as ' the Messiah ' (Mark 8. 29). The original meaning of ' Messiah ' was one anointed, and so consecrated, to a holy office; thus Saul is ' the LORD's anointed' in 1 Sam. 26. 11. Here then, the prophet means that Cyrus, though he does not know the LORD (as is said in 45. 4), is nevertheless the instrument in His hand to accomplish His will; just as the first Isaiah had said the same of Sennacherib (Isa. 10. 5–15; pp. 70–1 above). Cyrus overthrew the Babylonian empire in 538 B.C. But it is the LORD God Himself who will 'redeem' His people; and here the same Hebrew word which is used in Exod. 6. 6 and 15. 13, of the 'redemption' from Egypt, comes again in Isa. 41. 14; 43. 14; 44. 6, 24; 48. 17; 49. 7, 26, and elsewhere.

We are compelled to say that the prophet was mistaken, as regards the time. So were other prophets after him, who likewise believed that the Day of the LORD was near, and some psalmists also. The hope of the Return of the LORD to fill the Temple with His Presence was not fulfilled when the exiles returned to Jerusalem and rebuilt the Temple. We believe that it, with the other elements of the Messianic Hope, was fulfilled when Jesus came. Certainly it is to these prophets of the Exile that our Lord and His Apostles regularly go back to explain what it was that was happening in the events of the Gospel; and if the Messianic Hope was not fulfilled in Him, then it has never been fulfilled, but remains as 'a hope which failed'. But if it was indeed fulfilled in our Lord, that means that the LORD God kept His people waiting a long time; we, as we look at the history, can see that those centuries were for the Israel of God an important period of discipline.

Were they then sustained through this time of discipline by a hope which was mistaken? No: for the substance of the hope was not mistaken; and it is always the duty of the faithful in the Israel of God to believe in His saving Purpose, and look forward to a time when that Purpose shall be complete. Since the Purpose is God's Purpose, it is bound to be greater than our limited minds can take in : we are to face the future in hope, believing in God. So our Lord says : 'Watch, for ye know not the day nor the hour' (Matt. 25. 13). Those servants of God in the Old Testament period looked for an Event which did not come when and as they expected it. But the God in whom they hoped had not forgotten His purpose ; nor had He forgotten them, for we are assured in the New Testament that the Old Testament saints who prepared the way for our Lord's Kingdom, do enter into it : they with us, and we with them (Heb. 11. 39, 40). Similarly our Lord spoke of Abraham, Isaac, and Jacob as 'in the Kingdom of God' (Matt. 8. 11 ; Luke 13. 28).

(5) THE HOPE FOR ALL NATIONS

Long before the Exile, the Israelites had realized that Yahweh the God of Israel was interested in people of other nations, being indeed the one true God. Naaman the Syrian sends to Elisha the prophet of Israel to be healed of his leprosy, and becomes convinced that 'there is no God in all the earth, but in Israel' (2 Kings 5. 15). Amos believes that Yahweh who brought Israel out of Egypt had no less brought the Philistines from Caphtor and the Syrians from Kir (9.7). Isaiah receives a request from the 'Ethiopians' who live far away up the river Nile, for an oracle (chapter 18). His book, and those of Jeremiah and Ezekiel, contain quite a large number of prophecies addressed to the surrounding nations.

But it was during the Exile that it became clear (first, as it seems, to Second Isaiah) that because Yahweh the God of Israel was the creator of all men, therefore the knowledge of Him that Israel had received must be for all men. We have already quoted (p. 12) the great text of 45. 22–3, that because He is God and there is none else, to Him every knee shall bow, every tongue shall swear. But when, and how ? The

Servant of the LORD, according to Second Isaiah, was to do it; that is, (in so far as the Servant is Israel) this missionary apostolate is Israel's true vocation, and also that (in so far as the Servant is One who is to come) the fulfilment of this vocation is something that God will bring about when His time comes.

Elsewhere the coming in of the Gentiles is explicitly connected with the future Day when God comes to save His People, and the age of miracles begins again. This connexion is clearly made, for instance in Ps. 102, and in Zech. 2. 10–13. Often it is not clear what part the Gentile nations are to play in that great Day. In Isa. 60. the light is seen shining on Jerusalem, and the Gentiles are seen coming, bringing home the scattered Israelites; they provide transport (verses 4, 9), they offer their gifts (verses 6, 9, 13), they build the walls (verse 10), they bow themselves down before them (verse 14). Yet it seems that the Gentiles are perfectly content and quite happy, now that God's glory is revealed. In other places it is said that they will have a share in Israel's religion, and pray and offer sacrifice: Isa. 56. 6–8 (they will become proselytes); 66. 18–21.

It is not said that the Jews are to go out into all lands as missionaries. The coming in of the Gentiles is seen as a movement to a centre. The Sanctuary at Jerusalem is the centre of Israel's unity; it is to become the centre of unity for mankind.

Therefore it is always the Gentiles that come to Jerusalem. They are seen moving towards the Centre. This is the case in the earliest prophecy on this subject (Isa. 2. 2–4):

The mountain of the LORD's house shall be established in the top
    of the mountains
And shall be exalted above the hills,
    And all nations shall flow unto it.

And many peoples shall say,
Come ye, and let us go up to the mountain of the LORD,
  To the house of the God of Jacob;
And he will teach us of his ways,
And we will walk in his paths,
For out of Zion shall go forth the Law
And the word of the LORD from Jerusalem.

So it is throughout the Old Testament. And though in the New Testament the apostles go out as missionaries far and wide, yet the principle holds: for their message is still, 'Come to the Centre of unity for mankind'; and that centre is now not Jerusalem, nor the Temple, but Christ. He is the centre of unity for Jew and Gentile, as St. Paul works out in detail in the second chapter of the Epistle to the Ephesians: 'He is our peace, who hath made both [Jew and Gentile] one, and hath broken down the middle wall of partition' [the boundary wall surrounding the inner court and sanctuary in the Temple, past which no Gentile might go, under pain of death] . . . 'for through Him we both [Jew and Gentile] have access in one Spirit unto the Father' (Eph. 2. 14, 18).

Similarly in St. John's Gospel, the Jews are puzzled over the saying of Jesus, 'Whither I go, ye cannot come' (7. 34; cf. 13. 33-4), and wonder whether He will 'go to the Dispersion among the Greeks, and teach the Greeks' (7. 35). This does not happen in this gospel; what does happen is that Greeks come and seek to see Him (12. 20-1). For this was what was really happening wherever the Christian missionaries went out. He had given His life to bring the other sheep which were not of the Jewish fold, into the one Flock (10. 16), and to gather together in one the children of God that were scattered abroad (11. 52).

A. G. Hebert, *The Throne of David*. Faber, 1941. (Chs. II and III.) (Morehouse.)

CHAPTER IX

' *The Law was our schoolmaster* '

HAGGAI, ZECHARIAH, NEHEMIAH, EZRA

WE must now collect together some scraps of information about the period of the later Exile and the Return ; a period in which things of great importance were happening, and yet there is no written history. We are now in a position to answer the question, why they never wrote the history of the Exile, as they wrote the history (in itself much less important) of the Kings of Judah and Israel. It was because they needed to study the pre-exilic history, in order to know how they had sinned and had incurred God's just punishment. Nothing was more important than that they should repent of that sin, and avoid it for the future. Of their life in Babylon, there was nothing to record : better forget it : oh, that it might soon be over ! For the time was coming (oh, that it might be soon !) when history would begin again, when the LORD God would take action to redeem His people. Then there would be a new Book of the Exodus to write.

About the history of this period very much is uncertain. The books of Ezra and Nehemiah contain authentic memoirs, written by these two great men : they originally formed the continuation of Chronicles (for the beginning of Ezra repeats the conclusion of 2 Chronicles), and were edited by ' the Chronicler '. Scholars agree in distrusting the Chronicler as a historian, and most hold that Nehemiah came before Ezra, and that Nehemiah 8–10 really belongs to the story of Ezra.

THE EVENTS OF THE RETURN

The events of which we know may be summarized thus :

(a) c. 538 B.C. : Ezra 1–4. Return of a party from Babylon, led by Sheshbazzar (Ezra 1. 11), with the goodwill of
Cyrus : they restore the altar, but work on the Temple is
stopped, by order (chapter 4). This party may have been
stirred up to activity by Second Isaiah.

(b) c. 520–516 B.C. : Ezra 5–6, Book of Haggai, and Zechariah 1–8. The 'seventy years' after the Fall of Jerusalem
being now nearly completed (cf. Jer. 25. 12 ; 29. 10), these
two prophets urged the people to restore the Temple (would
it be done in time for the LORD's coming ?) : also, as it
seems, they believed that Zerubbabel the son of Shealtiel was
to be the Messianic King foretold by Isaiah (9. 1–7 and
11. 1–9) and Jeremiah (23. 5 and other places) : see Hag. 2.
1–9, 20–3 ; Zech. 4. 6–11. But in Zech. 3. 1 and 6. 11, it
looks as if Zerubbabel has disappeared, and Joshua son of
Jehosadak the high-priest is to be crowned instead. Certainly it seems that this was 'a hope that failed'. We do
not know what happened. It is possible to guess that
Zerubbabel was proclaimed King of Israel, in hope of a
divine intervention in accordance with the prophecy, and that
the Governor of Syria intervened. Possibly also Joshua was
set up after him, as 'a priest upon his throne' (Zech. 6. 13).
But this was not to be the Day of the LORD ; nor was the
way of temporal kingship His way.

(c) We have no more dates for some seventy years after
this, though there were some prophecies during this period ;
perhaps parts of Isa. 56–66, and almost certainly the Book of
Malachi, which is earlier than Nehemiah and by no means
the latest prophetic book of the Old Testament.

(d) Nehemiah visited Jerusalem twice, from 445 to 433

(Neh. 2. 1 ; 13. 6), and a second time after 433 (13. 7–31). His work was to rebuild the walls, against constant opposition (chapters 4 and 6) and put up a strong protest against violations of the letter and spirit of the Law (13. 7–14, 15–22, 23–31).

(e) Ezra came to Jerusalem with a strong body of returning exiles (Ezra 7. 1–7) 'in the seventh year of King Artaxerxes' of Persia : i.e. probably Artaxerxes II, date 397 B.C. (But the Chronicler, taking it that it was Artaxerxes I, and the date therefore 458 B.C., places Ezra before Nehemiah.) Ezra on his arrival conducted a 'purge', compelling Jews who had married pagan wives to break their marriages and send the wives away (Ezra 9–10).

Probably the next document in the history is Nehemiah chapter 8, where Ezra reads before the people the Book of the Law (Neh. 7.73 – 8.2), which he had brought from Babylon (Ezra 7. 14) ; he reads from a pulpit of wood, the people answer 'Amen', and the Levites explain what has been read (Neh. 8. 3–12). Some three weeks later (9. 1) there is another assembly, at which the Levites intone a solemn liturgical prayer (9. 5–38) in which they recount the dealings of the LORD with Israel from the beginning, declaring His faithfulness and their disobedience, and in verse 32 commending their cause into His hands ; finally in verse 38 they make a Covenant, and put their names to it (10. 1–27 gives the list of names). They promise 'to walk in God's law which was given by Moses the servant of God, and to observe and do all the commandments of the LORD our God, and His judgments and His statutes' (10. 29), not entering into mixed marriages (30), keeping the Sabbath (31), and undertaking a fixed charge to pay for the Temple services, with regular offerings of firstfruits of crops and cattle (32–9).

THE REFORM OF EZRA

That which was happening was an event of the greatest importance in the history of the Israel of God. By the Covenant made under Ezra the Mosaic Law, as it now stands in the Pentateuch, became binding. This was the inauguration of post-exilic Judaism. The importance of Ezra in the history is attested by the great place which he has taken in Jewish tradition, and by the legends which gathered round his name. There is a queer story in a book of the Apocrypha that all the books of the Law and the Prophets, indeed the whole Old Testament, were destroyed at the Fall of Jerusalem, and the whole was miraculously revealed to him, and written out (2 Esdras 14. 37–48).

The truth that lies behind this legend seems to be that Ezra was responsible for the canonization of the five ' Books of the Law ', as we have them, from Genesis to Deuteronomy : and at the solemn Covenant it was either these five Books, or the revised collection of laws which we call ' the Priestly Code ' that was accepted by Israel. 224 years before, King Josiah and his people had made a Covenant, and Deuteronomy had become Scripture. Before that date, 621 B.C., no canonical Scripture had ever existed : ' scripture ' began when that book, containing its testimony to the redeeming work of God in history and a comprehensive collection of laws, with exhortations to love and serve God truly, became an authoritative book, accepted by Israel as bearing the authority of God. Now, under Ezra, four more books were added : Genesis, containing the Creation-epic and the early stories, and Exodus, Leviticus and Numbers containing the narrative of the Exodus, and the ' priestly ' law. Josiah's Covenant was made shortly before Israel entered on its agony of suffering and death; Ezra's, after it had come out alive.

This Covenant was a great confession of faith. In the prayer in Neh. 9 they declared that God had redeemed them of old, and had throughout their history been faithful and true, but they had been unfaithful, and had been punished for it ; and they came to Him as a believing and penitent nation, which had learnt the lesson of the Exile, and purposed to walk from henceforth in His holy ways. They stood to the faith of Israel in the LORD God who had redeemed their forefathers out of Egypt close on a thousand years before. Therefore their Book of the Law must begin with a historical record.

THEIR ATTITUDE TO HISTORY

Yet it is easy for us to think of the men of that age—those who canonized the Pentateuch, those who had edited it in Babylon some years earlier, and those who had written the Priestly Narrative—as having no sense of history at all. It is this stratum of the narrative that gives us the ages of the patriarchs (Methuselah, 969), but almost wholly lacks the charming narrative style of the pre-exilic writings ; that spoils Moses for us by making him a man of eighty at the time of the Exodus, and expects us to think of between two and three million Israelites as finding subsistence in the desert, the fighting men being 600,000. All the laws, including those drawn up during the Exile, are ascribed to Moses. Then there is the Tabernacle in the wilderness, which could scarcely have been transported from place to place without a fleet of lorries on caterpillar tracks.

Certainly they lacked our curiosity in historical matters, which makes us wish to reconstruct the events of the past in all possible detail, and learn exactly how it happened. They would have been as much at a loss to understand the purpose of our inquisitiveness, as are the primitive peoples of the South Seas to understand the anthropologist who wants to ferret out all the details of their ancestral customs. Our idea of ' the disinterested search for knowledge for its own sake ' would be as much of an enigma to them as the secularized university which promotes it. They belonged to their own time, not to ours.

Yet it would be quite untrue to say that they had no sense of history. Even if they did not draw up their chronologies on the basis of careful investigation, but made them up on a scheme of their own, their minds went back over the past centuries ; and the thing for which they deserve most credit is that they preserved in the book the oldest and most authentic accounts, written before the Exile, even when these were flagrantly inconsistent with their newly-written ' priestly ' account. Nothing would have been easier than to suppress the old narratives, and keep only the ' priestly ' narrative, which probably they liked better. Their reason can only have been a clear perception that, because the LORD God really had redeemed them out of Egypt, therefore the old records of the history must be preserved.

Why did they attribute all the laws to Moses ? Because it had always been the tradition to do so ; the so-called Book of the Covenant (Exod. 20.23 – 23.19), dating from the early or middle Monarchy, and Deuteronomy, had been ascribed to Moses as a matter of course, just as all Psalms were reckoned as David's, and wisdom-books (Proverbs, Ecclesiastes, and the Wisdom of Solomon in the Apocrypha) were ascribed to Solomon. In each case there was a historical foundation : Moses must certainly have given laws and other teaching about Israel's duty to the God who had entered into Covenant with it : David no doubt wrote Psalms (no scholar doubts that the Lament over Saul and Jonathan in 2 Sam. 1 is a genuine work of his), and Solomon was certainly famed for his proverbs (1 Kings 4. 29–34). Similarly the whole tradition of Law grew up with Moses (as it were) for patron saint. And more : though Moses belonged to the remote past, the Covenant of the LORD God with Israel was a present fact for every Israelite. When he faced up to his duty to the Covenant-God, Moses was in a sense still speaking to him.

Why did they produce that account of the elaborate and unwieldy Tabernacle in the wilderness (Exod. 25–30, 35–40) ? Did they believe that it actually had been so ? If not, was it for them to re-write history as they chose ? The true account of the matter seems to be this : first, that the old pre-exilic document contained an account of a Tabernacle or Tent of Meeting, with the youthful Joshua as attendant (Exod. 33. 7–11) : there the Ark was kept. Second, that the ' priestly ' writers had their eye not only on the LORD's action in the past, but on His action in the future, when He would return ' to dwell in the midst of the children of Israel for ever ' (Ezek. 43. 7) in the restored Temple. When they read the old story of the Exodus, they thought of the second Exodus which the prophets had promised ; they were in Babylon, and they hoped that when they entered Palestine the LORD in His visible presence would lead them in. When they described the Tabernacle, their thoughts were full of the restored Temple where the LORD would dwell : and so they drew the design of the Tabernacle after the likeness of the Temple, and projected their own restored Temple-worship into the wilderness-period. Why ? Because they needed to assert that, as their faith in the LORD God was one with the faith in Him which Israel had held from the beginning, so the worship which they would hold in the restored Temple would be one with the worship of Israel from the beginning, when His Presence had been in their midst. The return of that Presence to dwell in the restored Sanctuary was that for which they longed.

As then all their Law was 'the Law of Moses', so in drawing out the plans for the restored Temple in the form of orders given by Moses for the construction of the Tabernacle, they were associating themselves with the founder of their religion, and going back to its sources. There had been a time, before the entry into Canaan, when as the prophet said, Israel had been 'holiness unto the Lord' (Jer. 2. 3). Since then there had been the great apostasy, when Israel had fallen away into idolatry, and become paganized. For this Israel had been terribly punished. But now a penitent Israel was seeking to return to her first love, and 'make answer as in the days of her youth, and as in the day when she came up out of the land of Egypt' (Hos. 2. 15). The Wilderness-period and the Entry into Canaan were being enacted over again, by an Israel which had been through God's discipline, and learnt great lessons at a terrible cost.

THEIR ATTITUDE TOWARDS THE GENTILE WORLD

Similar considerations will throw light on these horrible 'purges', in which Nehemiah and Ezra turned adrift numbers of women from surrounding countries who in all innocence had married Jewish husbands. We read in Neh. 13. 24 of wives from Ashdod, Ammon, and Moab ; ' and their children spake half in the language of Ashdod, and could not speak in the Jews' language, but according to the language of each people'. The same was brought to Ezra's notice when he first came into the country (Ezra 9. 1–3) ; and it nearly broke his heart. We can read in his memoirs his agonized and shame-stricken prayer. This was the very sin for which God had visited His people with that terrible punishment. And now, when it seemed that Israel was penitent and forgiven, and there was real hope of a new start, there had come this awful relapse, on the part even of some who had returned from exile (9. 4).

At the evening oblation I arose up from my humiliation, even with my garment and my mantle rent; and I fell upon my knees, and spread out my hands unto the LORD my God; and I said:
'O my God, I am ashamed and blush to lift up my face to thee, my God: for our iniquities are increased over our head, and our guiltiness is grown up to the heavens. Since the days of our fathers we have been exceedingly guilty, unto this day. . . . And now for a little moment grace hath been showed from the LORD our God, to leave us a remnant to escape, and to give us a nail in his holy place, that our God may lighten our eyes, and give us a little reviving in our bondage. . . . And now, O our God, what shall we say after this? for we have forsaken thy commandments, which thou hast commanded by thy servants the prophets. . . . And after all that is come upon us for our evil deeds, . . . shall we again break thy commandments, and join in affinity with the peoples that do these abominations? Wouldest thou not be angry with us till thou hadst consumed us, so that there should be no remnant, nor any to escape? (Ezra 9. 5–15).

For the Israelite's home was the place where the children were to be taught in the ways of the LORD (Deut. 6. 7): repeatedly in the Law it is said that the children would ask, for instance, about the Passover, 'What mean ye by this service?' and the answer is given (Exod. 12. 26). But now paganism was being admitted into the home itself; pagan mothers, knowing no better, would bring up the children in a pagan way. There was no help for it: this evil must be stopped at once, however painful the process. In Ezra 10 we read how they spent days and days going into individual cases. Nehemiah, it is to be feared, had been far less patient (Neh. 13. 25, 28).

It was a painful duty, but it had to be done. Yet questions rise. Had not the Second Isaiah spoken a century or more earlier, of the conversion of the Gentiles to believe in the God of Israel? Does this turning adrift of the Gentile wives mean that there had been a sad falling-away from that earlier ideal? Then, Israel was to stretch out its arms and include the Gentiles: now, it was busy pushing them away and excluding them.

It can well be that there was something in this. The author of the Book of Jonah, writing perhaps not long after Ezra, bitterly satirizes the Jews of his day for their harsh attitude towards the Gentiles.

In this tale Jonah, though commanded to speak in God's name to the people of Nineveh, takes ship in the opposite direction, to the far west (1. 1–3). God sends a violent storm; in the storm, the pagan sailors show up much better than Jonah; they pray to their respective gods, while he retires to his bunk to sleep (verses 5, 6). He has told them that he is running away from God, and that they will have to throw him overboard; they row hard in order not to have to do this, but at last Jonah has to go. The storm at once moderates; the men 'feared the LORD exceedingly, and they offered a sacrifice to the LORD, and made vows' (1. 10–16). Clearly there was good in these Gentiles. As for Jonah, he must now resume his errand (3. 1–3); the result is a remarkable response on the part of the Ninevites (3. 4–10). Jonah is disgusted, and tells God so:

But it displeased Jonah exceedingly, and he was angry. And he prayed unto the LORD, and said, 'I pray thee, O LORD, was not this my saying, when I was yet in my country? Therefore I hasted to flee to Tarshish; for I knew that thou art a gracious God and full of compassion, slow to anger, and plenteous in mercy, and repentest thee of the evil.' (4. 1–2.)

Finally, peevish and petulant Jonah is annoyed because the gourd which shelters him perishes; but if Jonah is grieved about the gourd, on which he has bestowed no labour, shall not God care about the people of Nineveh who are His own creatures? (4. 10–11.)

Another book which is held to have been, if not wholly written, at least re-edited, about this time, is the Book of Ruth. Deuteronomy had said that an Ammonite or Moabite must not enter into the assembly of the LORD, to the tenth generation (Deut. 23. 3), and the prohibition was quoted and used by Nehemiah (13. 1, 2). But this charming tale of Ruth tells of the good and faithful Moabite girl who marries an Israelite husband, and becomes the great-grandmother of no less a person than David himself (Ruth 4. 17).

But here is the strange thing. The faith of Israel that the LORD God of Israel is the one true God leads to two opposite conclusions. He alone is God: therefore all nations whom He has made must come at last to worship Him (Isa. 45. 22–3; Ps. 86. 9–10). He alone is God: therefore Israel which He has called to know Him, must beware lest it be drawn away from him into idolatry (cf. the First Commandment). An idolatrous and paganized Israel would deserve God's judgement (Ezra 9. 13–14), and would be of no use in witnessing for God to the Gentiles.

But in truth God's time had not yet come. The prophecies of Isaiah had .looked forward to the coming Day of the LORD, the time when His glory would be revealed, the age of miracles would begin again, and what was now impossible would become possible. In actual fact, it was impossible for Israel to do more than gather in a few proselytes out of some neighbouring nations; and these converts had to leave their own nation behind, in order to enter the Jewish nation. The Day had not yet come when it would be possible for the

Greek to remain a Greek and the Roman a Roman, and as such be gathered into the New Israel, the Church.

Therefore when St. Paul went out on his missionary work, what he found in every city was this : that round the Jewish community that worshipped in its synagogue there was a fringe of pagans who were powerfully attracted by the teaching about God which they found there, and the worship, and the high standard of morals, and yet were unable to become members of the Jewish community. They were attracted by this Jewish faith, because here they found a belief and a religious practice which demanded to be taken seriously, and as such was an entirely new thing in their experience ; yet they could not come within the fellowship of this wonderful religion without leaving their own nation and becoming Jews. This can be illustrated from several places in the New Testament : the crowd of non-Jewish worshippers at Pisidian Antioch (Acts 13. 44–9), Cornelius the Roman soldier, a devout man of prayer and almsgiving, and friendly with the Jews (Acts 10. 4, 22, 30–1), whom St. Peter baptized, and the other Roman centurion who had built for the Jews a synagogue (Luke 7. 4–5). It is this fact that accounts for the very rapid growth of the Church in the Apostolic age : everywhere there were pagans whom Judaism had touched but was unable to bring within its fellowship.

We ought not then to blame Nehemiah and Ezra for losing sight of the noble 'universalism' of Second Isaiah, as if it were simply a matter of ecclesiastical narrow-mindedness. If they and their successors had been broad-minded, tolerant and lax, their Judaism would have lost its cutting edge, and have lost at the same time its power to attract the Gentiles. For here was a religion which was exclusive because it believed in a Real God, who had made a Covenant with His People, and imposed on them a weekly Sabbath-day, and abstinence from forbidden foods, and a high moral demand; and at the same time a God whom it proclaimed as the Creator and the God of the whole earth.

Israel was being pulled in two directions at once. The problem of the Gentile world was one which it could not solve. No solution was possible till the Messiah had come, and God's Purpose for Israel had been completed.

For the history:

W. O. E. Oesterley and T. H. Robinson, *The History of Israel.* Oxford, Clarendon Press, 1942. (Vol. II, pp. 42–141.)

The Clarendon Bible, Vol. IV: *Israel after the Exile*, by W. F. Lofthouse. Oxford University Press, 1928.

D. Batho, *The Birth of Judaism.* S.P.C.K. (Macmillan.)

A more general discussion in:

H. H. Rowley, *The Rediscovery of the Old Testament.* James Clark, 1945. (Ch. VII, 'The Rise of Judaism'.)

CHAPTER X

' LORD, what love have I unto thy Law '

CHRONICLES, PROVERBS, DANIEL, PSALM 119

SOME time in the fourth century, perhaps about 335 B.C., the Samaritans separated from the Jews of Jerusalem and built a rival temple at Gerizim (referred to in John 4. 20) ; this was destroyed by the Jews in 109 B.C.   In 331 B.C. the Persian Empire came to an end, when Alexander the Great brought the whole of the Middle East under Greek rule.   In the years following 169 B.C. Antiochus Epiphanes attempted to establish throughout Syria a uniform standard of Greek culture : the refusal of the Jews to accept this brought the Maccabean persecutions, and the successful revolt of Judas Maccabeus. The period of the rule of the high-priests followed, till in the middle of the first century B.C. the Middle East fell under the Roman Empire.   These four sentences, describing the external history, give us four convenient divisions for our study of Israel's religious life.

THE TEMPLE WORSHIP

Chronicles, Ezra and Nehemiah, written about 300 B.C., form a complete history from Adam onwards ; but the first nine chapters consist of little more than lists of names, till in 1 Chron. 10 the narrative begins with Saul's defeat on Mount Gilboa.   From this point onwards, the narrative is mainly based on the Books of Samuel and Kings.   But the story is strangely fanciful ; the Chronicler is mainly interested in the ritual of the Temple worship, and a comparison of 1 Chron. 15 and 16 with 2 Sam. 6 shows that he is relating the story of the bringing of the Ark to Zion by David as he thinks it should have been done. In 2 Chron. 13 there is a quite impossible story about a battle between King Abijah of Judah and Jeroboam of Israel, in which the latter, though outnumbering his enemy two to one, is defeated with half a million casualties. After Jeroboam's reign the northern kingdom almost disappears from the narrative, which confines itself to the history of Judah : the reason is that to the Chronicler the name 'Samaria' suggests the Samaritan schism, and the rival temple.

To the historian, such fanciful writing must seem to be a falsification of history ; and the Chronicler can well be accused of ecclesiastical and ritualistic narrow-mindedness. The other side of the account is that he has a truly wonderful sense of the dignity and glory of liturgical worship, and of 'the beauty of holiness' in the sanctuary. His liturgical descriptions, such as 2 Chron. 5, are wonderful : and there is nothing finer of its kind, perhaps, in the whole Bible (except in the Book of Revelation) than the following act of praise, put into the mouth of David :

Blessed be thou, O LORD,
The God of Israel our Father,
　For ever and ever.
Thine, O LORD, is the greatness, and the power,
And the glory, and the victory, and the majesty :
　For all that is in the heaven and in the earth is thine :
For thine is the Kingdom, O LORD,
And thou art exalted as head above all.
Both riches and honour come of thee,
And in thine hand is power and might,
And in thine hand it is to make great,
　And to give strength unto all.

Now therefore, our God, we thank thee
   And praise thy glorious Name.
But who am I, and what is my people,
That we should be able to offer so willingly after this sort?
   For all things come of thee,
   And of thine own have we given thee. (1 Chron. 29. 10–14.)

The narrow-mindedness which we see in the Chronicler is typical of those in all ages who are in love with religion, and easily forget that the whole world belongs to God, and that God is interested not only in religion but in all that men do and suffer. But this narrow-mindedness is not typical of the Old Testament; and in this post-exilic period books were written in a spirit of conscious protest against it. The Book of Job discusses the problem of undeserved suffering, and firmly rejects the accepted doctrine, stated by Job's friends, that happiness is proportioned to well-doing and punishment to sin. Job is a 'free-thinker' in a more radical sense than those people to-day who take that title to themselves; and the book ends, not with a triumphant statement of orthodox doctrine, but by Job being confronted with God Himself. The study of the book of Job requires a commentary that sets out the course of the argument in a more detailed way than could be even attempted here.

THE PRAISES OF WISDOM

From the end of the fourth century onwards the Middle East lay open to Greek influence, which affected the whole of life, manners and morals as well as thought. Above all in Alexandria the Jew came in contact with the Greek; it was here that the Greek Bible, called the Septuagint (*LXX*) was produced. Some of the books of the Old Testament, chiefly Proverbs and Ecclesiastes, bear deep marks from this contact, and all the books of the Apocrypha; for these books, mostly written originally in Greek, are those which appear in the Greek Bible and not in the Hebrew. This approach to the Greeks was made in the Wisdom-literature.

Proverbs is a book of this type, and contains probably some ancient material; Solomon was renowned for 'wisdom', and was credited with three thousand proverbs (1 Kings 4. 32). But Proverbs, in its final form, belongs to the Greek period. In the first seven chapters we find a series of fervent moral exhortations, addressed to the Jewish young man surrounded by the new temptations to immorality which met him on every side in the free life of the Greek cities. These chapters are not occupied with 'conventional morals': they were written to meet the urgent need of young men in great moral danger.

> My son, if thou wilt receive my words,
> And lay up my commandments with thee;
> So that thou incline thine ear unto wisdom,
> And apply thine heart to understanding . . .
> Then shalt thou understand the fear of the LORD,
> And find the knowledge of God . . .
> For wisdom shall enter into thine heart,
> And knowledge shall be pleasant unto thy soul . . .
> To deliver thee from the way of evil,
> From the men that speak froward things;
> Who forsake the paths of uprightness,
> To walk in the ways of darkness . . .
> To deliver thee from the strange woman,
> Even from the stranger that flattereth with her words;
> Which forsaketh the friend of her youth,
> And forgetteth the Covenant of her God;
> For her house inclineth unto death,
> And her paths unto the dead:
> None that go to her return again,
> Neither do they attain to the paths of life. (Prov. 2. 1–19.)

We are thus introduced to the figure of 'Wisdom'. Wisdom is more than a human quality, nor is she a kind of personification of 'Education'; she is the divine Wisdom, God's voice speaking to man and apprehended by his reason and conscience. She stands at the entry of the city, calling to the sons of men (Prov. 8. 3, 4): speaking of uprightness and truth, and the forsaking of evil ways (5–14): standing behind the just rule of kings, bestowing wealth and well-being (15–21). But more: Wisdom existed from the first creation of the world, and was in God's mind, or was His 'master-workman', when He laid the foundations of the earth. Therefore he who rejects the voice of Wisdom sins against the truth of his own being:

The LORD possessed me in the beginning of His way,
Before his works of old.
I was set up from everlasting, from the beginning,
Before ever the world was . . .
    When he established the heavens, I was there,
    When he set a circle upon the face of the deep . . .
    When he gave to the sea its bound,
    That the waters should not transgress his commandment;
    When he marked out the foundations of the earth,
Then I was by Him, as a master-workman,
And I was daily his delight,
Rejoicing always before him,
Rejoicing in his habitable earth,
    And my delight was with the sons of men.
Now therefore, my sons, hearken unto me,
For blessed are they that keep my ways. (Prov. 8. 22–32.)

Here indeed something is being said. As in Babylon the Jewish writer had produced an epic of creation, so in contact with this new Greek world they return to this theme of creation. The Greek nation had produced the philosophers, who had speculated about the origin of things, and laid the foundations of natural science. To them this teaching about the divine Wisdom would appeal ; and we notice how strong the emphasis on morals is made, for there was need for it. Another Wisdom-text is Job 28 ('Where shall Wisdom be found ? and where is the place of understanding ? ' Answer : God, who has set in order the whole universe, has ' established it and searched it out ' ; and to man the word is, that ' the fear of the LORD is Wisdom, and to depart from evil is understanding '.)

Ecclesiasticus, written by Joshua ben Sira about 180 B.C., expresses a similar conception of Wisdom ; but it is given a new turn. Among all the nations of the world Wisdom chose Israel to be her dwelling-place ; in Jerusalem was her authority ; there, in Israel, she took root and brought forth fruit. Wisdom's voice is heard :

I came forth from the mouth of the Most High,
And covered the earth as a mist.
I dwelt in high places,
And my throne is in the pillar of the cloud . . .
In the waves of the sea, and in all the earth,
And in every people and nation, I got a possession.
With all these I sought rest ;
And in whose inheritance shall I abide ?
Then the Creator of all things gave me a commandment,
And he that created me made my tabernacle to rest, and said,
   Let thy tabernacle be in Jacob,
   And thy inheritance in Israel. (Ecclus. 24. 3–8.)

In verse 23 she is identified with the Mosaic Law. But Wisdom is inexhaustible, for ' her thoughts are filled from the sea, and her counsels from the great deep ' (28–9) ; and the study of Wisdom leads on to more and more (30–4).

In Wisdom 7 (date some time after 100 B.C.), Wisdom is

no longer seen as personal, but rather as a spirit or effulgence proceeding from God (7. 25, 26), and His instrument in the work of creation (22); thus to man there has come his wonderful knowledge of God's world, in the sciences of physics and astronomy (17-19), zoology, meteorology, botony, and medicine (20). But Wisdom also bestows spiritual gifts:

She is an effulgence from everlasting light,
    And an unspotted mirror of the working of God,
       And an image of his goodness.
    And she, being one, hath power to do all things,
       And, remaining in herself, reneweth all things;
    And from generation to generation passing into holy souls
       She maketh men friends of God and prophets.
For nothing doth God love save him that dwelleth with Wisdom.
For she is fairer than the sun,
    And above all the constellations of the stars;
Being compared with light, she is found to be before it;
    For to the light of day succeedeth night,
    But against wisdom evil doth not prevail;
But she reacheth from one end to another with full strength,
And ordereth all things graciously. (Wisdom 7.26 – 8.1.)

All this was a fruitful expansion of the older statements of the doctrine of creation. And because the Christian Gospel is the announcement that God has redeemed that same human nature which He created in the beginning, the work of these Wisdom-writers is used in the New Testament, to throw light on the person of Jesus the Son of God. The Wisdom-writers, meditating on God's created world, worked out the thought of the expression of God's glory in His works generally and in man; the Wisdom of God has produced the pattern on which physical nature and human nature are modelled. Then Jesus came; His work was to restore the true pattern of human nature, delivering it from the dominion of Satan, of sin, of selfish pride, and calling men to be converted and become like little children; of all this, the human character of Jesus Himself is the pattern. So then: if salvation through Jesus Christ is real salvation, and the true and original pattern of human nature is restored, then He who came from God bringing this salvation is none other than the Divine Wisdom, through which (or through *whom*) God created the world. This is what is said in the Prologue of St. John's Gospel, where in place of *Sophia*, Wisdom, St. John speaks of the *Logos* or Word of God:

> In the beginning was the Word,
>   And the Word was with God,
>   And the Word was God.
> All things were made by him
> And without him was not anything made that was made.
> (John 1. 1–3.)

FAITHFULNESS UNTO DEATH

But Judaism had a different sort of contact with Greek thought when Antiochus Epiphanes ('the Magnificent') sought to impose throughout Syria and the countries dependent on Antioch a uniform pattern of Greek civilization: 'that all should be one people, and that each should forsake his own laws' (1 Macc. 1. 41–2). The programme was accepted everywhere. It was attractive, it was up-to-date; and among the peoples of the Middle East no one found any sufficient reason for refusing to march in the path of progress. If it meant building temples and offering sacrifice to an additional god or two in addition to those already worshipped, what of that? Where there are many gods, there is always room for one more: except only in Israel.

For there was one nation which believed in one God only,

and that He was the true God, and had called Israel to be His People—and it mattered. The New Order required that in the Temple set apart for His worship sacrifices should be offered to Zeus and Aphrodite, the Sabbath be disregarded, the food-rules of the Law be set aside (1 Macc. 1. 44–9); besides, all sorts of strange foreign customs were brought in, a Greek Gymnasium or sports-ground was made, and all the traditions of Israel's life were broken. For the New Order, so generously tolerant of all religions, could not tolerate a religion which was treated seriously because it rested on the worship of the one true God.

Hence a systematic persecution began: heathen altars appeared everywhere in Palestine, copies of the Book of the Law were confiscated and burnt, and those who refused to conform, and women who had their babies circumcised, were put to death.

And many in Israel were fully resolved and confirmed in themselves, not to eat unclean things; and they chose to die, that they might not be defiled with the meats, and that they might not profane the holy covenant: and they died. (1 Macc. 1. 62–3.)

Some of them fled into the wilderness; the king's forces pursued them there, and prepared to attack them on the Sabbath day, first offering amnesty and free pardon if even now they would conform: they refused, and a thousand, including women and children, were massacred on one day (2. 29–38). There is another story in 2 Macc. 6. 18–7, of seven sons of one mother, who gave their lives, one after another, as martyrs for the faith. There followed the armed rising under Judas Maccabeus, a heroic struggle in which a succession of foreign armies were defeated, and an independent Jewish state set up.

But we are concerned with the persecution and the martyrdoms, which are alluded to in the splendid panegyric on the heroes of the faith in Heb. 11. 33–8 ; a passage which was an unconscious prophecy of the persecutions of the Christians which began about the time when the Epistle to the Hebrews was written, and continued, on and off, for 250 years, till at last the victory was won and the Roman Empire became Christian :

Who through faith subdued kingdoms, wrought righteousness, obtained promises, stopped the mouths of lions [like Daniel], quenched the power of fire [like the Three Children in Dan. 3], escaped the edge of the sword, from weakness were made strong, waxed mighty in war, put to flight armies of aliens [like Judas Maccabeus]. Women received their dead by a resurrection : and others were tortured, not accepting their deliverance, that they might obtain a better resurrection ; and others had trial of mockings and scourgings, yea moreover of bonds and imprisonment ; they were stoned, they were sawn asunder, they were tempted, they were slain with the sword : they went about in sheepskins and goatskins, being destitute, afflicted, evil intreated (of whom the world was not worthy), wandering in deserts and mountains and caves, and the holes of the earth. (Heb. 11. 33–8.)

But the first of the persecutions was this Maccabean persecution. Now we see another side of the ' exclusiveness ' which we were discussing in the last chapter. Loyalty to the Faith in the one true God made this exclusiveness necessary. Now the test came ; and Israel was found faithful, even unto death.

The history of it is recorded in the Apocrypha. But one book of the Old Testament belongs to this period, and was written to sustain the faith of the martyrs in their conflict : the Book of Daniel. This book purports to be a story of events in the time of Nebuchadnezzar, four hundred years before : but its actual reference is to this persecution. The great story of the Burning Fiery Furnace was written to describe the New Order which Antiochus Epiphanes set up, to which all peoples, nations, and languages were required to conform under pain of death (Dan. 3. 4–6). The style of this chapter is purposely formal and stilted; perhaps we can discern a tone of mockery in the enumeration of the state officials and civil servants, and that of the musical instruments —both repeated several times; but the grim reality behind them is that of the totalitarian state and a culture imposed by threat of force:

Nebuchadnezzar the king made an image of gold, whose height was threescore cubits [88 feet] and the breadth thereof six cubits; he set it up in the plain of Dura, in the province of Babylon. Then Nebuchadnezzar the king sent to gather together the satraps, the deputies, and the governors, the judges, the treasurers, the counsellors, the sheriffs, and all the rulers of the provinces, to come to the dedication of the image which Nebuchadnezzar the king had set up . . . Then the herald cried aloud, 'To you it is commanded, O peoples, nations and languages, that at what time ye hear the sound of the cornet, flute, harp, sackbut, psaltery, dulcimer, and all kinds of music, ye fall down and worship the golden image that Nebuchadnezzar hath set up; and whoso falleth not down and worshippeth shall the same hour be cast into the midst of a burning fiery furnace.' (Dan. 3. 1–6.)

The three faithful Jews refuse to conform. They say:

Our God whom we serve is able to deliver us from the burning fiery furnace; and he will deliver us out of thy hand, O king. But if not, be it known unto thee, O king, that we will not worship thy gods, nor worship the golden image which thou hast set up. (17–18.)

They are then thrown into the furnace (20–3); we are to understand that they died. But the story goes on that they are seen loose, walking in the midst of the fire ; and in the midst of the fire there is seen with them Another, and the fire has no power over them (24–8). ' Others were tortured,' says the Epistle to the Hebrews, ' not accepting their deliverance, that they might obtain a better resurrection ' (Heb. 11. 35).

For it was now that the Jews learnt to believe in the resurrection of the dead. The Old Testament, up to this point, had no clear doctrine of a future life. But these martyrdoms made it clear that those who had loved God enough to lose their lives for His sake, had not lost their lives in losing them ; ' God is not the God of the dead, but of the living ' (Mark 12. 27).

The other chapters of the Book of Daniel all become intelligible in this context. ' Nebuchadnezzar ' represents the persecuting heathen power : he boasts of his worldly greatness, saying ' Is not this great Babylon which I have built ? ' (4. 30). But those whose faith is set in the living God have the secret of a divine kingdom which is real and permanent. In the story of Belshazzar and the Writing on the Wall in chapter 5, judgement is pronounced on the worldly tyrannical power. In chapter 6, Daniel, whose rule of life includes prayer to God three times a day (6. 10 ; cf. Ps. 55. 17), is thrown to the Den of Lions, and is delivered. In the vision of the Son of Man in chapter 7, there are seen four terrible beasts, representing the world-empires which had oppressed the Israelites, the Assyrian, the Babylonian, the Persian, and lastly the Greek (7. 3–8) ; but then is seen the throne of God, and the figure of the Son of Man :

I saw in the night visions, and behold, there came with the clouds of heaven one like unto a Son of man, and he came even to the Ancient of days, and they brought him near before him. And there was given him dominion, and glory, and a kingdom, that all the peoples, nations and languages should serve him : his dominion is an everlasting dominion, which shall not pass away, and his kingdom that which shall not be destroyed. (Dan. 7. 13–14.)

Then the vision is explained : the emphasis is all laid on the last and most terrible of the beasts (the persecuting King Antiochus), who will ' make war with the saints and prevail against them ' (21), and will ' speak words against the Most High, and he shall think to change the times and the Law ; and they shall be given into his hand until a time, and times, and half a time ' (25). Those to whom the prophecy is addressed will suffer helplessly ; but the matter is in God's hands, and their suffering will be only for as long as He allows. The last word lies with Him, and at the last His servants shall possess the Kingdom (26–7).

THE RIGHTEOUSNESS OF THE LAW

The period of the Maccabean persecutions saw the beginning of the ' sect ' (or rather, party) of the Pharisees, as a clearly-marked group within Judaism. We ought not to think of the Pharisees as ' hypocrites ' making an insincere profession of religion, unless we are prepared to judge ourselves as well as them by that standard which our Lord applied. Judged by our ordinary standards, they were and remained good and decent men, in sharp contrast with the Sadducees, the party which followed the worldly tradition of the Maccabean High-Priests. The Pharisees believed in God, and accepted for themselves the discipline of their personal lives by the Mosaic Law.

Pharisaism at its best is represented by the wonderful 119th Psalm, which is indeed likely to have been written some considerable time earlier, before the great persecution, but which expresses more perfectly perhaps than any other writing in the Old Testament the regulation of the individual

life by a personal rule of obedience to God at which the
Pharisees aimed.

> Thou hast dealt well with thy servant,
>   O LORD, according to thy word.
> Teach me good judgment and knowledge;
>   For I have believed in thy commandments.
> Before I was afflicted I went astray;
>   But now I observe thy word.
> Thou art good, and doest good;
>   Teach me thy statutes. (Ps. 119. 65–8.)

In each of its 176 verses there occurs the word 'law',
'testimonies', 'judgements', or some synonym. Yet this
psalm is not legalistic, for it breathes the spirit of a humble
and sincere devotion, and expresses delight and joy in seeking
to follow the way of God's will. Indeed, this psalm may
be said to sum up that which Israel was set to learn above
all during the post-exilic period: namely, the personal
training-up of the Israelite in the way of the devout life,
under the influence of the Synagogue.

If we look back four or five centuries, we can see how
great had been the advance. In Babylon during the Exile,
there had been a small remnant of faithful Israelites diligently
setting themselves to repent of the sins which the prophets
had condemned. A hundred years later, about 450 B.C.,
Malachi had castigated the slovenliness of the temple service
at Jerusalem: any maimed or lame animal was good enough
for sacrifice. Ezra's reforms altered all that; but it was
necessary to deal very sharply with the mixed marriages which
brought pagan ways into the Jewish home. Now, in the
later post-exilic period, the Temple sacrifices were performed
punctually and reverently. There were synagogues everywhere, in Jerusalem and all over Palestine, and outside

Palestine in Babylonia, Egypt, Asia Minor, and all the places where Jews lived: there, Sabbath by Sabbath, the people were instructed in the Law, and trained in habits of devotion. Israel as a whole had become a religious society, with its centre in Jerusalem and its branches spreading far and wide over the world. The old idolatry which the prophets had condemned had ceased to exist. So far as religion was concerned Israel had become more deeply than ever before the people of the LORD; and a very great part in this transformation had been played by the patient work of the scribes, who Sabbath by Sabbath had instructed the people in the ways of true religion.

Yet it was still the Law, and not the Gospel; the prophetic promises of the Messianic Age had not been fulfilled. The prophets had looked forward to a Day of the LORD, when the age of miracles would begin again, and the LORD would come to dwell among His people in His Sanctuary, and His Spirit would be poured out, and all things would become new. One generation after another had hoped for the coming of that Kingdom: when the Book of Daniel was written to uphold the faithful in the persecution, it had seemed that the Day was very near. Some believed that it would come with the appearance of a Saviour from heaven, to bring the present world-order to an end, to abolish all evil, and inaugurate the Reign of God in righteousness. The common expectation of the Pharisees, however, was expressed in the Psalms of Solomon, about 44 B.C.: that by Divine intervention a Kingdom of Israel would be set up in this world; Israel would be supreme among the nations, and would be ruled by a godly king, the 'Messiah' or 'the Lord's anointed', who would himself be a model of godly living and would rule the nation, and the world, in righteousness. The Pharisees hoped and prayed that, in response to the godliness and faithfulness of His People, God would hasten the time. The Zealots, who formed the right wing of the Pharisaic party, were hoping for another Judas Maccabeus and another holy war, to bring victory to Israel and inaugurate the new age.

But was the new age, the promised Messianic Reign, to bring forth an Israel devoted to a minute observance of religious rules? And was another side of it to be the imperialism of a nationalistic Israel, ruling other nations with a rod of iron? When we recall the meaning which had been attached by Jeremiah and Ezekiel to the promises of the New Covenant and the outpouring of the Spirit of the LORD (see pp. 102–5 above), it becomes apparent that this later Judaism had fallen away from that higher vision. It had faithfully preserved the outward forms of its religion ; but it had fashioned a notion of the Messiah according to its own ideas, and it was not ready for Him whom God would send.

E. Bevan, *Jerusalem under the High Priests*. E. Arnold, 1904.
(Longmans.)

CHAPTER XI

'The time is fulfilled'

THE GOSPEL

AND then He came.

St. Mark's Gospel, the first of our Gospels to be written, begins by quoting two prophecies. The first is from Mal. 3. 1: 'Behold I send my messenger before Thy face, which shall prepare Thy way before Thee.' This is the passage which continues 'And the LORD, whom ye seek, shall suddenly come to His temple, even the Messenger of the Covenant whom ye delight in. . . . But who may abide the day of His coming, and who shall stand when He appeareth? For He is like a refiner's fire and like fuller's soap'—see Mal. 3. 1–6. The second is from Second Isaiah, chapter 40: 'The voice of one crying in the wilderness, Prepare ye the way of the LORD, make His paths straight.' This is the prophecy which begins 'Comfort ye, comfort ye my people, saith your God,' and continues 'The Glory of the LORD shall be revealed, and all flesh shall see it together: for the mouth of the LORD hath spoken it'—see Isa. 40. 1–11.

Then comes a summary account of the preaching of John the Baptist in the wilderness; and then the coming of Jesus to be baptized by John in the Jordan, and the vision which He saw of the heavens being rent asunder (Mark 1. 10: 'O that Thou wouldest rend the heavens and come down,' Isa. 64. 1) and of the words addressed to Him: 'Thou art my beloved Son, in Thee I am well pleased ' (' Behold My servant whom I uphold ; My beloved, in whom My soul delighteth,' Isa. 42. 1).   Then after forty days of solitude in the wilderness, Jesus begins His ministry with the words, ' The time [looked forward to by the prophets] is fully come, and the Kingdom [or Reign, or Kingly Rule] of God is at hand [or, has drawn near] : repent, and believe the Gospel [the Glad News] '—Mark 1. 15.

It is the age of miracles beginning again.   That which had been impossible now becomes possible.   We will continue with St. Mark, chapter 1 : He goes into a synagogue ; a man possessed by an evil spirit is restored to health and sanity.   Peter's mother-in-law is healed of a fever.   He speaks to the people, and they are amazed, for He teaches ' with authority ' and not like the scribes who preached because there had to be a sermon that day, but as one who bears a message that must be delivered.   He comes, bringing deliverance and liberation to men : ' the blind receive their sight, the lame walk, the lepers are cleansed, the deaf hear, the dead are raised up, and the poor have the Gospel preached to them ' (Matt. 11. 5 ; Luke 7. 22) ; men are saved and healed in body and in soul, and the words in which this is expressed are an echo of Isa. 35. 5–6 : ' Then the eyes of the blind shall be opened, and the ears of the deaf be unstopped ; then shall the lame man leap as a hart, and the tongue of the dumb sing.'

So He goes round Galilee, preaching the Gospel of the Kingdom of God, and teaching in parables.   But the scribes are soon stirred up to opposition (Mark 2.1 – 3.6) : twice we hear of a deputation from Jerusalem, to watch the new movement (3. 22 ; 7. 1), and at 7. 23 the Galilean ministry comes to an end.   For a time now He is mostly outside Galilee (7.24 – 9.50).   During this period He asks the Twelve whom they believe Him to be, and Peter confesses that He is the Messiah. He immediately speaks of Himself as the Son of Man, and says that the Son of Man must suffer and be rejected and after three days rise again. After this, three Disciples see Him transfigured on the mount with Moses and Elijah, and hear similar words to those which He had heard at His baptism; only now the words are addressed to them. He enters Judaea (10. 1) on the way to Jerusalem; He enters Jerusalem in state as King, not as a warrior-king on a war horse, but as the peaceful King of whom the prophet Zechariah had spoken, riding on an ass (Zech. 9. 9–10). Then He cleanses the Temple, His Temple over which He has authority; this is a direct challenge to the Chief Priests, and after this events move swiftly. After He has celebrated the Last Supper with His disciples, in which He interprets His death as sacrifice, He is arrested and tried before the Sanhedrin; the decisive question is whether He claims to be the Messiah, the Son of God (14. 61). He replies ' I am : and ye shall see the Son of Man sitting on the right hand of power [i.e. of God] and coming with the clouds of heaven.' He is brought before Pilate, condemned, and crucified with the title over His head ' The King of the Jews ': He is buried, and on the third morning His tomb is found empty, and the message is given that He is risen from the dead.

After fifty days, at the Feast of Pentecost, the disciples, who in the gospel narrative confess that at His passion they all failed Him, are found proclaiming to Israel, in the very place where He had been condemned to a shameful death, that God had reversed that sentence. ' The Day of the LORD has arrived. What you see happening is the fulfilment of Joel's prophecy (Acts 2. 17–21). You all know about the ministry of Jesus :

Jesus of Nazareth, a man approved of God by mighty works
and wonders and signs, which God did by him in the midst of
you, even as ye yourselves know : him, being delivered up by
the determinate counsel and foreknowledge of God, ye by the
hands of men without the Law [the Roman governor] did crucify
and slay : whom God raised up, having loosed the pangs of death :
because it was not possible that he should be holden of it (22–4) ;

and God has vindicated Him as the promised King who
should sit on the throne of David (30–1). Of His resurrection we His apostles are witnesses ; and the present gift
of the Spirit is the sign that Jesus sits now at God's right
hand (32–5, quoting Ps. 110). Therefore let all the house
of Israel know assuredly that God hath made Him Lord
and Messiah, this Jesus whom ye crucified ' (36).

The substance of the discourse ascribed to St. Peter here
comes again in several other speeches in the early part of
Acts (esp. 3. 12–26 ; 10. 34–43 ; 13. 16–41) ; and recent
scholarship has reached the definite conclusion that these
accounts of the earliest Christian preaching are primitive and
authentic. They show a common outline, of which the
main points are : The time looked forward to by the Prophets
is come : the promised Deliverer is Jesus of Nazareth ; you
rejected Him : but God has vindicated Him by raising Him
from death : and He is exalted now as King : therefore
repent, believe, be baptized.

The apostolic preaching, both here and throughout the
New Testament, is that through Jesus Christ the Purpose
of God for man's salvation reaches its completion, that
purpose which God took in hand when He first chose Israel
to be His people ; the form which this would take had
been announced, as regards its main features, by the great
prophets of the Exile. We analysed above this Messianic
Hope into five chief points : that there would be (i) a Second

Exodus: (ii) A New Covenant: (iii) an outpouring of the Spirit of the Lord: (iv) a return of the LORD to dwell with His People: and (v) the extension of these blessings to all nations.

We will now follow out the fulfilment of these predictions. Yet it is no mechanical fulfilment. Something great and new appeared in the world when Jesus came ('Behold, I make all things new,' Rev. 21. 5; and verily He did). The predictions of the prophets are not, as it were, history written in advance. Christians have often taken them so, but it is mischievously false to treat the Old Testament prophecies like the predictions in Old Moore's Almanac. In fulfilling them, He transforms them.

Yet there is a real fulfilment. The prophet, taught by God, was seeking to discern the direction in which God's saving Purpose was moving. No prophet's insight was deep enough to grasp the whole of God's Purpose: different prophets saw different sides of it. St. Peter in his Epistle pictures the prophets as seeking and striving to understand what the Spirit of the Messiah was teaching them to see, about the sufferings of the Messiah and the victory to which they would lead (1 Pet. 1. 10–11). The first words of the Epistle to the Hebrews are that God, who spake at sundry times and in divers manners, in many fragments and in many styles or modes, through the prophets, has at the end of that pre-Messianic period spoken to us once for all in His Son (Heb. 1. 1). The prophets had a true but incomplete insight into God's Purpose. This our Lord and His apostles acknowledge by the way in which they refer to the prophets; and it is remarkable that it is chiefly to the great prophets of the Exile that they go back.

Let us then consider in order the five headings which we used in chapter VIII.

THE SECOND EXODUS

The original Exodus had been a deliverance from oppression in Egypt; the Second Exodus, to which Jeremiah and Second Isaiah looked forward, was to be a return home of the exiles deported to Babylonia—in both cases a deliverance from political oppression. The Exodus which our Lord accomplished at Jerusalem was not a deliverance from external enemies, but the liberation of man himself from his real Enemy, namely Sin, the love of the self, Satan, death and the fear of death. It is not the liberation of men from the bondage or constraint put on them by other men who are able to tyrannize over them: it is the radical and final liberation of men themselves from their condition of powerlessness to control their own lives. It is not the setting-free of men from outward constraint, so that now they can do as they please, and enjoy their leisure time as they choose; it is the inward liberation of the will, to be able to do what they would always have been glad to do, if only they could.

The first Isaiah had indeed prophesied of a future King ' of the stock of Jesse ', who would sit on David's throne at Jerusalem and rule in righteousness; and the expectation that the Messiah would be an earthly king holding temporal power persisted, though it seems that the fate of Zerubbabel indicated that this was not God's way; the Pharisees in our Lord's day looked forward to such a king. On the other hand, the great prophets of the Exile spoke chiefly of an Israel wholly converted to seek God's will, rather than an Israel exalted to a position of political supremacy.

It is plain from the gospels that our Lord faced this question, particularly in His temptation on the Mount, when the Devil offered Him the kingdoms of this world, and the glory of them:

The devil taketh him unto an exceeding high mountain, and sheweth him all the kingdoms of the world, and the glory of them; and he said unto him, 'All these things will I give thee, if thou wilt fall down and worship me.' Then said Jesus unto him, 'Get thee hence, Satan: for it is written, thou shalt worship the LORD thy God, and him only shalt thou serve.' (Matt. 4. 8–10.)

There is here one point that needs explanation. It is clear that the account of the three temptations must have been given to the disciples by our Lord Himself: and that He expressed the spiritual conflict in symbolical terms (something like the representation of political issues in the cartoons which appear in our papers)—indeed, this is the clearest way in which these things can be expressed. When, therefore, He tells us that the Devil came to Him, with the offer of the kingdoms of the world, we ought not to imagine Him spending a large part of the forty days making up His mind to do what He knew was right, and to reject the Devil's offer. Rather, the conflict consisted in finding out that it actually was the Devil's offer. It *was* the Devil who suggested this: but temptations do not come with labels tied on to them. That the Messianic King should seek temporal power was a specious and attractive possibility. But the conclusion of our LORD's conflict was the clear understanding that this was in fact a temptation of the Devil; and we ought to think that, when He saw it to be such, He immediately set it aside.

For it was attractive. To establish a righteous kingdom, such a kingdom as had never existed before in the world's history, with just laws and righteous judgement: to set up an Utopia on earth. And it was within His power. But He rejected it with the words, 'Thou shall worship the LORD thy God, and Him only shalt thou serve', from Deut. 6. 13. Such a kingdom, in its earthly glory and success, would not be the Reign or Kingly Rule of God, but a caricature of it and a substitute for it. It would not be the Kingdom of God, but one of the kingdoms of the world.

What way, then, did He follow instead? What did He actually do and say? It was not that He gave up the seeking of a Kingdom, or ceased to think of Himself as King; it was that the Kingdom was God's Kingdom, and the word and the idea needed to be re-interpreted in a different sense, and implemented in a different way. The thing which was to happen was that the LORD God should reign over men, reign over their hearts and minds and wills, and men return to an attitude of entire obedience to Him. This would be a very different thing from an earthly kingdom in which the Messiah held the temporal power.

Once two disciples came to Him seeking to be promised the chief places in His Kingdom. He replied that they did not know what they were asking for; were they prepared to drink of His cup and be baptized with His baptism? (Mark 10. 35–8.) He followed this up with some words to all the Twelve about the nature of authority. ' The rulers of the nations use their authority as an opportunity to domineer over men; but that is a false notion of their calling, contrary to the truth. In My Kingdom the true principle is to be acted upon: namely that the ruler is the general servant of all, called to bear the burdens of all. Of this the pattern is the Son of Man, who came not to be ministered unto but to minister, and to give His life a ransom for many ' (Mark 10. 42–5). The corollary of this equation of authority with service is that the Son of Man is the King of kings.

On His disciples He made an unqualified demand for loyalty and obedience to Him; yet that demand rested simply on obedience to the truth. To them He was no despot, fascinating them with His personality and robbing them of their freedom : for in being His disciples they became free and became truly themselves :

If ye abide in my word, then are ye truly my disciples : and ye shall know the Truth : and the Truth shall make you free (John 8. 31–2).

But this was possible for them only on the basis of the most radical self-criticism. For the Lord insisted on digging right down in the human soul till He came to rock-bottom ; and this meant the exposure of all vanity, self-deceit and wishful thinking, particularly of the religious variety. Seen in this very searching light, the Pharisees, who were the religious people of the day, appeared as ' hypocrites ' : it was not that they were playing a double part and pretending to be righteous when they were not (for the Hebrew and Aramaic word did not mean that), but that inwardly and in their secret hearts they were not godly men. ' I know you, that ye have not the love of God in yourselves ' (John 5. 42). On the other hand, many ' sinners ' (women of loose lives ; men who were outcast from decent society through working as ' publicans ', or tax-collectors), when they were faced with the same exposure of the secrets of their hearts, accepted it and found forgiveness and peace. Such was the ' woman who was a sinner ', who anointed His feet in the house of Simon the Pharisee. Simon was shocked, and said in his heart :

' This man, if he were a prophet, would have perceived who and what manner of woman this is, that she is a sinner.' But Jesus answering said unto him, ' Simon, I have somewhat to say unto thee.' And he said, ' Master, say on.' ' A certain lender had two debtors ; the one owed him five hundred pence, and the other fifty. When they had not wherewith to pay, he forgave them both. Which of them therefore will love him most?' Simon answered and said, 'He, I suppose, to whom he forgave the most.' And turning to the woman, he said unto Simon, ' Seest thou this woman? I entered into thine house, thou gavest me no water for my feet: but she hath wetted my feet with her tears, and wiped them with her hair. Thou gavest me no kiss; but she, since the time I came in, hath not ceased to kiss my feet. My head with oil thou didst not anoint: but she hath anointed my feet with ointment. Wherefore, I say unto thee, Her sins, which are many, are forgiven, because she loved much; but to whom little is forgiven, the same loveth little.' And he said unto her, ' Thy sins are forgiven.' (Luke 7. 39–48.)

So He went among men, proclaiming the Kingly Rule of God, and meaning what He said. He had come, as He put it, longing to gather together the people of Israel ' as a hen gathereth her chickens under her wing' (Matt. 23. 27), that Israel might be truly the People of God, under the leadership of Him whom the Father had sent. It was the fulfilment of all that to which the Old Testament had been moving, the consummation of its whole spiritual development, the accomplishment of the Purpose of God for His chosen people. The LORD whose way had so long been prepared, had come; the LORD to whom the Temple belonged had suddenly come to His Temple (cf. the prophecies quoted in Mark 1. 2, 3, p. 141 above).

To the Temple, then, He came. His entry into the city on Palm Sunday appears to have been planned by Him to correspond with the terms of a famous prophecy which spoke of Jerusalem's King coming to her, lowly and riding on an ass, and declared that this king would cut off the battle-bow and the war-horse, and would speak peace to the nations, and exercise universal rule (see Zech. 9. 9–10). Had He

regarded Himself as destined for temporal power, He would
have been on a war-horse. Next day He entered the Temple,
and expelled the traders who held a market there, changing
foreign into Jewish money and selling animals for sacrifice.
It was not merely that He saw an evil thing going on and
intervened to stop it; it was that He had come to His Temple,
where He as God's chosen had authority, and it was His
part to cleanse it of the evil that was going on in it. That
this is so is proved by the immediate reaction on the part
of the Chief Priests; they asked Him outright 'By what
authority doest thou these things?'

By entering Jerusalem in state and by assuming authority
in the Temple, He had posed the Chief Priests, and the
people generally, with a question which demanded an answer.
Would they acknowledge Him as the promised King of
Israel? Or would they destroy Him? It must be one or
the other. No evasion was possible.

They had Him crucified, by sentence of Pontius Pilate, in
order that He might die the death to which a particular
curse was attached—'he that is hanged [on a tree] is accursed
of God', from Deut. 21. 23—so that every Jew who heard
of it would say that this Jesus was an impious pretender
to the highest of all functions, on whom God had broken
out, causing Him to be denounced by His High-Priest and
condemned to that accursed death. But His disciples, who
on that Good Friday night were completely broken men
(for the meaning of the curse attached to the cross could not
escape them), tell us of the tomb being found empty on the
third day, and how they saw Him risen, and how within
seven weeks they were proclaiming, in the very city where
He had been crucified, that God had raised Him from the
dead, reversing the sentence which men had pronounced.
The Gospel was true : this was the promised King. God

had established His kingdom, in spite of the resistance of rebellious men. God's love had proved stronger than human hate. No power of earth or of hell could prevent the 'Stone which the builders rejected' going into its place as the corner-stone (Mark 12. 10). As for the 'curse', it was impossible that it should take effect on the Divine Saviour, on whom rested the fulness of the Divine Blessing. And so St. Paul explains, quoting the text from Deuteronomy which he had been accustomed to apply to Jesus when he was Saul the Pharisee, the persecutor of the Christians:

Christ redeemed us from the curse of the Law [which we men had brought on ourselves by disobeying God's Law] having become a curse for us (for it is written, Cursed is every one that hangeth on a tree); that upon the Gentiles might come the Blessing of Abraham, in Christ Jesus; that we might receive the Promise of the Spirit, through faith (Gal. 3. 13–14).

In St. John's Gospel it is made plain that the Crucified is the true King. In John 18. 36 it is explained that His Kingdom is not of (from) this world: if it were, He would have an army and a police to protect Him: and in verse 37 that He is the universal spiritual King, who is come to 'bear witness unto the truth'—the truth about God, and about men, and about every man, you and me. In 19. 14 Pilate shows Him to the Jews: 'Behold, your King'; and they, in order to disown Him, are compelled to say that they have no King but Caesar. Nothing remains then but that Jesus should be crucified; and He is crucified with the title over His head 'Jesus of Nazareth, the King of the Jews', written in the three languages which mattered in the ancient world (verses 19–20). If Jesus had claimed temporal power, His Crucifixion would be the final repudiation of that claim. But if His Kingship was what He said it was and what He proved it to be in His relations with His disciples, His royal claim and His kingly character are in no way affected by what His enemies did to Him ; rather, He when He is lifted up from the earth, draws all men to Himself (John 12. 32).

Such is our Lord's Kingship, and such His authority. Here we see how the Christian Church becomes different from Old Israel. Old Israel was called to bear witness to God's spiritual claim, but its spiritual authority was confused with the temporal authority of its civil rulers, whenever it was an independent state. The Christian Church exists in all nations side by side with the civil power ; but it can never rightly hold the temporal power, since it becomes false to its own nature whenever it tries to do so. Its regular teaching is that the civil ruler rules by God's ordinance. Men must 'render unto Caesar the things that are Caesar's, and to God the things that are God's' (Mark 12. 17)—in other words, there is a duty owed to Caesar, but not an absolute duty, for there are things that are not Caesar's. This is the principle that the State transgresses when it becomes totalitarian, and claims control over men's minds and consciences : for man's mind and conscience are created to respond to God's truth, and of that truth the Church is sent to bear witness, in Christ's name (John 18. 37). Church and State have their respective functions, and each needs the other.

Thus Christ is King, but not as holding temporal power : just as the Second Exodus is a Redemption or deliverance not from political oppression, not from enemies who rob man of his political freedom, but from the Enemy who robs man of his personal freedom, making him the slave of his lusts, and the slave of his pride. The question with which Jesus posed the Chief Priests when He cleansed the Temple remains the one question which finally matters. He stands before us and all men as the Universal Spiritual King : will we have Him ?

THE NEW COVENANT

Jeremiah had foreseen a New Covenant, not like the Old Covenant made when Israel came out of Egypt, but one that would make Israel truly to be the People of God, when they should all know Him, and His Law would not be learnt by them at second-hand, but would be written in their hearts, and their sins would be forgiven (Jer. 31. 31–4 : pp. 102–3 above). To this Jesus referred when, according to the earliest written record of the Last Supper, He said ' This cup is the New Covenant in My blood ' (1 Cor. 11. 25). ' His blood ' is His sacrifice ; by His sacrificial death the New Covenant promised by Jeremiah is now inaugurated, and the Eucharistic chalice is the sacrament of this. St. Paul refers to the New Covenant in 2 Cor. 3, where he says that his Corinthian converts need no epistle or document of commendation from him ; they themselves are his epistle, an epistle written not in ink on paper, but with God's Holy Spirit in human hearts, and not like the Old Covenant on tables of stone, but in tables that are hearts of flesh (2 Cor. 3. 3). St. Paul himself is a minister of this New Covenant, not of the letter but of the Spirit (verse 6) : the ' letter ' is the written Mosaic Law.

Jeremiah had looked forward to a Day when the Law of God would be written in the people's hearts (and the word Law, *Torah*, means not merely written rules but instruction, teaching, guidance), and they should truly know Him. Other prophets spoke of the Spirit of the LORD being given —that is to say, the LORD coming to dwell with His people, in their hearts, bringing new power, and making things possible which previously were impossible. But till that

Day came, what was there for it but to follow the teaching of the prophets and the other men of God, to follow a rule of life such as Daniel's prayer three times a day, and observe the rules of worship and the other rules laid down in the Mosaic Law ? Since the reform of Ezra the outward shape of the life of Israel had been more or less firmly fixed : there was the Temple with its priesthood, the synagogue, the scriptures of the Law and the Prophets, the Tradition of the Elders by which the Mosaic Law was expounded and applied, the liturgical year with its festivals and fasts and the weekly Sabbath—all this was the outward vesture of Israel's spiritual character as the People of God.

Yet for the Israelite it was and remained a system of observances. The scribes worked hard in the synagogues to keep lazy people up to a minimum standard of observance ; others, more religiously gifted, kept a high standard of observance. The standard of righteousness was there in the Book, in the splendid examples of the lives of the men of God, in the precepts of the wise men, in the rules of the Law, and it was up to each man to live up to this standard as far as he could and would. Those who did best could scarcely avoid comparing themselves with others who did not fast twice a week and did not give tithes of all their income. They were better observers of the Law, they were better Israelites, than those laxer ones ; could they not take some credit for it, and feel that their conduct was meritorious ? Such was St. Paul before his conversion : ' circumcised the eighth day . . . a Hebrew of the Hebrews ; as touching the Law a Pharisee ; as touching zeal, persecuting the Church ; as touching the righteousness which is in the Law, found blameless ' (Phil. 3. 5–6).

Our Lord exposed this sort of thing quite mercilessly. He drew the gigantic grotesque of the Pharisee calling God's

attention to his own virtues ('God, I thank thee that I
am not as other men are', Luke 18. 11–12). It was self-
righteousness, it was spiritual pride; that whole attitude of
mind was monstrous and inhuman. When people sit in
judgement on others in that way, everyone else becomes
aware of their faults and judges them (Matt. 7. 1, 2). It is
contrary to the truth; the person who officiously insists on
removing a mote (speck) out of his brother's eye has got a
rafter in his own eye! (Matt. 7. 3). He who exalts himself is abased; he who humbles himself is exalted (Luke
14. 11).

The Pharisee ought to have known better; something
within him ought to have warned him. The Righteousness
of God was for him expressed in the Law and the teaching
that went with it; and what he had before his eyes was a
mental picture of the ideal Pharisee (himself) carrying out his
ideal of the godly life. Everyone who tries to serve God
knows what this temptation is.

But what difference did our Lord's coming make? This:
that the Righteousness of God is now exhibited, not in a
written law, but in a human life, in the Person of Jesus:

But now, apart from the Law, a Righteousness of God hath
been manifested, being witnessed by the Law and the Prophets:
even the Righteousness of God, through faith of Jesus Christ,
unto all them that believe (Rom. 3. 21–2).

No disciple of Jesus, going about with Him day after day,
could be self-complacent about his own virtues; and he
would find from time to time that the words of Jesus could
be like a sharp sword, pitilessly exposing his vanity and self-
conceit (see for instance Mark 9. 33–7, 38–41).

Then came His arrest, His trial, His crucifixion. We
might have expected that the gospel narratives would record

not only the Lord's patient endurance but the steady loyalty of His chosen followers. Instead we find them bravely announcing their readiness to follow Him to the end ('Lord, I am ready to go with thee to prison and to death,' Luke 22. 33), yet failing to pray in the Garden of Gethsemane (Mark 14. 34–42): when He was arrested they 'all forsook him and fled' (Mark 14. 50). This is not a sarcastic comment on the apostles' behaviour by an unfriendly critic: for the account comes from the apostles themselves, and is their confession of sin. After this they tell us how their leader publicly disowned Jesus three times in the presence of His enemies (Mark 14. 66–72).

On Easter morning Peter was one of the first to see the risen Lord: 'the Lord is risen indeed, and hath appeared to Simon'. In John 21. 15–17 he is asked by the Lord the searching question, three times over because of his threefold denial: 'Simon, son of John, lovest thou me?' After such an experience, what could be the ground of St. Peter's confidence that he was at peace with God? Not any self-complacency over his own good works, or other merits, or loyalty to our Lord: nothing except the fact that when he had lost his balance and had fallen heavily, the Lord had held him up. 'Blessed be the God and Father of our Lord Jesus Christ, who . . . begat us again unto a living hope [after faith and hope had been dead] by the Resurrection of Jesus Christ from the dead' (1 Pet. 1. 3, the first words of the Epistle, after the address).

We keep Good Friday and Easter every year; St. Peter's experience is that of us all. We have shared in the common sin of mankind, the sin which brought Jesus Christ to the death of the cross. But He died praying 'Father, forgive them'; and the Resurrection means that in dying He won the victory, and God's love is here shown as stronger than man's sin. 'Herein is love, not that we loved God but that He loved us' (1 John 4. 10). The attractive power of the cross is stronger than man's power to run away: 'I, if I be lifted up from the earth, will draw all men unto me' (John 12. 32).

This is what St. Paul means by 'Justification through Faith'. The Christian is made right with God, and is brought to be at peace with God, not in virtue of 'the works of the law', not through attaining any Pharisaic standard of religion and morals, not through any virtues or merits of his own, not through any religiousness of his own. He is brought to be at peace with God simply because Christ came as the Saviour of the world; and 'faith' means simply accepting this, and saying, 'I am a weak and sinful man, on whom God has laid His hand.'

So it is that when our Lord says at the institution of the Holy Eucharist, 'This chalice is the New Covenant in my Blood', the promised New Covenant is brought into existence through the sacrifice (blood) of the Messiah; and the Eucharist is the sacrament of His sacrifice. And that which has been effected once for all *for* us through the coming of the Saviour and His death and resurrection, must then be effected *in* us by the coming of the Holy Spirit.

THE GIFT OF THE HOLY GHOST

When we think of the Spirit of the LORD, or the Holy Ghost, we do best to keep in our minds the Biblical phrases, such as *Immanuel*, God with us. The Spirit of the LORD is the LORD present in power. We read in Judges 13. 24–5 how the young Samson grew up, 'and the LORD blessed him, and the Spirit of the LORD began to move him in Mahaneh-Dan'; how, after young David had been anointed by Samuel at the sacrificial feast at Bethlehem, 'the Spirit of the LORD came mightily upon David from that day forward' (1 Sam. 16. 13). The prophets spoke by the Spirit: one of them says 'I truly am full of power by the Spirit of the LORD, and of judgment, and of might, to declare unto Jacob his transgression, and to Israel his sin' (Mic. 3. 8). And then, the prophets announce that in the future Day of the LORD, the Messianic King will be filled with the Spirit of the LORD, the spirit of wisdom and understanding, of counsel and might, of knowledge and of the fear of the LORD (Isa. 11. 2; cf. 61. 1); and likewise the Messianic people will receive prophetic insight, seeing visions and dreaming dreams, according to Joel 2. 28, while according to Ezek. 36. 26-7, when the LORD 'puts his Spirit within' His people, He will 'take away the stony heart out of their flesh, and will give them a heart of flesh'—that is, a responsive and ready willingness to do His will.

Such is the gift of the Holy Spirit in the New Testament; the outward and visible sign that the Day has come, the Messianic Order has begun, even here and now on earth; the pledge or first instalment ('earnest', 2 Cor. 1. 22; Eph. 1. 14) of that which is to be given in its fulness in the future world, in the Church Triumphant, in what we call 'heaven'. When the Holy Ghost has been given, the emphasis is no longer, as with the Pharisees, on what men must do to serve God, but rather on faith in the presence of the Spirit—God with us—who makes all things possible. It is not, of course, that there is no longer any need to think out problems of conduct, or any need to have a rule of life: on the contrary, both these are necessary. 'Look carefully how ye walk, not as unwise but as wise; redeeming the time, because the days are evil' (Eph. 5. 15-16). 'Work out your own salvation with fear and trembling'—that is one side of the matter; the other follows immediately—

' for it is God that worketh in you, both to will and to work for his good pleasure ' (Phil. 2. 12–13).

But now comes a question : if the Holy Spirit was given at Pentecost, does that mean that throughout the Old Testament period He had been absent ? Does it mean that He is given to Christians only, and never to non-Christians ? that His light shines in the Church, but outside there is complete darkness ? Truly this would be a monstrous notion. But the question is one that takes some answering; and it will not do to say that the difference is simply one of degree—for here as always we need to be rather careful in using mechanical analogies, and we cannot safely describe the working of God the Holy Spirit by comparison with an electric current.

We say in the Creed that the Holy Ghost is ' the Lord and the Giver of Life '. Natural life and spiritual life all comes from Him as its source. All that is good in all men everywhere is the gift of God : it would be monstrous even to imagine any good anywhere that is not from Him. Even an atheist who denies God with his mind owes to Him all the good that is in him.

When we turn to the Old Testament, we find everywhere the thought of the presence of God in His world. The doctrine of creation does not mean that God, having brought the world into existence, leaves it to the operation of the laws of nature, like a man winding up a clock and leaving it to run by itself: that is the false notion of Deism, an invention of modern rationalism. God is present and active in nature :

He causeth the grass to grow for the cattle
And herb, for the service of man;
That He may bring food out of the earth,
And wine that maketh glad the heart of man (Ps. 104. 14–15).

He ' breathed into man's nostrils the breath of life, and man became a living soul' (Gen. 2. 7). It is He that ' teacheth man knowledge' (Ps. 94. 11).

But it is in the Prologue of St. John's Gospel that we find the clearest statement of the presence of God with men. By His Word ' all things were made' (John 1. 3), and ' in him was life, and the life was the light of men ', the light of reason and conscience (1. 4) : ' the light that lighteneth every man that cometh into the world' (1. 9). But though ' He was in the world and the world was made by him ', so that pagan man owed to Him everything, ' the world knew him not' (1. 10). Then in the fullness of time ' the Word was made flesh ', in the Incarnation of the Son of God (1. 14), and through Him it became possible for men to be born anew, to a new life, through believing on His name (1. 12–13).

The same distinction can be applied to the Holy Spirit. The Spirit, the Divine Life, is operative everywhere throughout the organic creation and in all men universally. The same Holy Spirit comes at Pentecost, as the Gift of the ascended Christ (Acts 2. 33), as the agent of God's ' new creation ' ; ' in one Spirit were we baptized into one body, whether Jews or Greeks, whether bond or free, and were all made to drink of one Spirit' (1 Cor. 12. 13). This is the outpouring of the Spirit on the Messianic people, of which the prophets of the Exile spoke : His coming means that God's saving purpose for mankind is now complete, and that the remedy for sin has been given through Christ's death and resurrection, and through Him men are reconciled to God.

We Christians of to-day have in general failed rather badly to understand and teach what the coming of the Holy Spirit means ; we fail worst of all when we interpret the work of the Holy Spirit in psychological terms. There is a hymn, not one of the best, which says 'Every virtue we possess, And every victory won, And every thought of holiness, are His alone.' When we think of the Holy Spirit, we commonly think of our own moral progress : not, perhaps, a very enlivening subject. But we ought to be thinking of Him, first, as the Lord and the Giver of Life throughout God's created order; and then as the agent of God's saving purpose for mankind, the source of the life of the Church, present and active in the sacraments, and making its glorious Gospel live in men's minds and hearts : *Immanuel*, God with us.

The gift of the Holy Ghost was explained by St. Peter at Pentecost as the sign that the promised Day of the LORD had come : God had accomplished His saving Purpose, and Israel was re-constituted as the Catholic Church for all nations. To-day in the Church the Holy Ghost brings forth supernatural fruits of grace, the love, joy, and peace which flow out from faith in God through Jesus Christ, and bind men together in unity on that basis. The Holy Ghost is God with us; His action is God's own action. 'The wind bloweth where it listeth ' in John 3. 8 ought to be translated (since 'spirit', 'breath' and 'wind' are one word in Greek) 'The Spirit breathes (inspires) where He wills, and thou [Nicodemus] hearest His voice' (seeing the effects in people's changed lives), 'but thou knowest not whence He cometh nor whither He goeth ' (not understanding that these are the effects of God carrying through His purpose of salvation in men's souls). There are unlimited ' diversities of gifts ' (1 Cor. 12. 4–11), for God never repeats Himself.

Always, however, in the New Testament the present gift of the Spirit is spoken of as the first-fruits or the first instalment (Rom. 8. 23 ; 2 Cor. 1. 22 ; 5. 5 ; Eph. 1. 14), of that which is to be given in its fulness in the World-to-Come, after the Second Advent; when God's saving Purpose, which is complete now as a work done *for* us, shall have been completed also *in* us, and the Kingly Rule of Christ be finally established.

THE TABERNACLING PRESENCE

Sometimes the prophets look forward to a human prince who shall sit on David's throne. More often they speak of the LORD Himself coming to save: rending the heavens and coming down (Isa. 64. 1); putting on His breastplate of righteousness and all the heavenly armour, and coming in person to fight His own battle (Isa. 59. 16–18), against the sin and evil in which men are quite hopelessly entangled (verses 9–14); as the Good Shepherd, Himself seeking out His sheep (Ezek. 34. 11–16). So Second Isaiah spoke of the LORD coming in power, and feeding His flock like a shepherd, gathering the lambs in His arms, gently tending the mothers with young (Isa. 40. 11); and the psalmist prays, 'Arise and help us, and deliver us for thy mercy's sake' (Ps. 44. 26).

His coming was to be the return of the Presence which had been manifested in the Pillar of Cloud, and had dwelt on the Sacred Ark: He would return to His Temple, and the House would be filled with Glory (Hag. 2. 7); He would dwell in the midst of His people (Zech. 2. 11); He would suddenly come to His Temple (Mal. 3. 1). There are several psalms which express this same thought. In Ps. 102, written in exile, the psalmist longs for the rebuilding of Zion and the appearing of the LORD in His Glory (verses 13, 15). In Ps. 126 it seems that they have had the great joy of the return from Exile: 'When the LORD turned again the captivity of Zion, then were we like unto them that dream'

(126. 1) ; but the Presence had not returned to the Temple, and they long for It to appear and the Messianic Day to dawn.

St. John speaks of the Return of the Presence in his Prologue : ' The Word was made flesh and *dwelt* among us, and we beheld his *Glory*' (1. 14). The word Glory is regularly used in the Old Testament to describe the Presence ; and the word ' dwelt ' recalls the phrase ' the place which the LORD shall choose to cause his name to dwell there' (Deut. 12. 5, 11, &c.). Indeed the consonants of the Greek verb which St. John uses, *eskēnōse*, reproduce the consonants of the Hebrew *shakhan*, to dwell ; *mishkhan*, the Tabernacle, *Shekhinah*, the Presence.

Yet the prophecies were not fulfilled literally. The Presence never returned to the sanctuary of that Temple whose outer court our Lord cleansed ; that Temple made with hands was destroyed by Titus in A.D. 70. St. John, quoting a saying which according to Mark 14. 56–9 was quoted against our Lord at His trial in a garbled form, and giving as its true form ' Destroy this temple and in three days I will raise it up ' (John 2. 19), adds the comment, ' But he spake of the temple of his body ' (verse 21). The place where the Presence dwelt was first the humanity of Jesus ; His body was raised from the dead after three days. It is also the Church which is His body : for it is this that is now the real Temple of God ; the people, not the church-building constructed of bricks and timber. The people are the Church. The people are the living stones of the Temple (1 Pet. 2. 5).

This teaching runs through the New Testament. Our LORD implied it when He spoke of Himself as the stone which the builders rejected, but which would become the head corner-stone (Mark 12. 10, quoting Ps. 118. 22–3). St. Paul is explicit : the Corinthian Christians are a Temple of God, and the Spirit of God dwells in them (1 Cor. 3. 16, 17); they are the Sanctuary in which the Presence dwells. In 2 Cor. 6. 16 he quotes, with a difference, a text from Lev. 26. 11, 12, in which God says that He will set His Tabernacle (*mishkhan*) *among* His People and walk among them: St. Paul has it, ' For we are a temple of the living God: even as God said, I will dwell *in* them, and walk in them.' In 1 Cor. 6. 19 each Christian's body is called a temple, because the Holy Ghost dwells there. But elsewhere it is the community that is the temple. In Eph. 2. 20-2 it is the whole Church universal, composed of Jews and Gentiles; built on the foundation of the apostles and prophets, Christ Jesus being the great corner-stone which underlies them; built up, by the building into it of all the members. In the vision of ' heaven ' in Revelation, there is no visible temple; ' for the LORD God Almighty and the Lamb are the temple thereof' (21. 22).

Once again, then, the prophecy is transformed in being fulfilled. There is a similar transformation in the idea of the sacrifices which were offered in the Temple. Under the old law a worshipper brought an animal or other prescribed offering; though prophets and psalmists told him that what God really wanted was that he should give himself to God to do His will. One psalmist understood that this was the real sacrifice, the reality of which the animal sacrifices were only a symbol:

Thou desirest no sacrifice, else would I give it thee;
Thou delightest not in burnt offerings:
The sacrifice of God is a troubled spirit;
A broken and a contrite heart, O God, thou wilt not despise
(Ps. 51. 16–17).

And Second Isaiah saw that the martyrdom of the Suffering

Servant had been ordained by God as a sacrifice for sin, acceptable to Himself (Isa. 53. 10).

So it was that our Lord, at the Last Supper, by using sacrificial words over the bread and wine, interpreted His death as the supreme Sacrifice: and so in the Eucharist the Church recalls and re-enacts this Sacrifice, and in it the communicants in being united to the Lord are themselves offered up in sacrifice, with Him and in Him.

As then the Temple of the Old Covenant finds its fulfilment in a temple built of human souls, and in these the Presence dwells; so the animal-sacrifices offered by men are fulfilled in the One Sacrifice of God's own Passover Lamb, and the worshippers cannot offer Him without themselves being offered up in Him. Yet there is a real continuity of idea. It is not that the idea found in the Old Testament is discarded, and something different substituted for it; our Lord is come not to destroy, but to fulfil, the Law and the Prophets (Matt. 5. 17); in Him we see that towards which the Old Testament is moving.

Therefore when we use the Old Testament, we do not have to discard phrases like Jerusalem, Zion, the sanctuary, or the priest's preparation for sacrifice (as in Ps. 26) or the description of the rite of the burnt-offering. We should have to discard them if they referred only to an order of things which had passed away. But we can use them if we know, as every Christian ought to know, how they are fulfilled in Christ and have become woven into the texture of Christian devotion. Thus, if we may dare to paraphrase Heb. 9. 11–14:

'Christ is the High Priest of the Messianic order: He offers His sacrifice in no temple made with hands, situated in this created world, but in the Heavenly Temple; and His Sacrifice is no oblation of the blood of goats and calves, but is His own blood; and He has entered in once for all into that Sanctuary, having won an eternal, not merely a temporal, deliverance. The effect of His Sacrifice is not such a cleansing from outward and ceremonial defilement as was effected by sprinkling the blood of bulls or goats or a heifer, but the cleansing and sanctifying of human hearts and minds to render to the living God that service which they owe Him, through the pure and sinless self-oblation of the Saviour in the power of the eternal Holy Spirit.'

THE COMING IN OF THE GENTILES

The prophecies of the coming in of the Gentiles to share Israel's faith come primarily in Second Isaiah, and then in Zechariah, and in several important psalms; they are illustrated in Jonah and Ruth. We have seen also how in Nehemiah and Ezra the need of guarding the integrity of Israel's faith and life led to an exclusiveness whose main object was to keep pagan influences out of the Jewish home; and how in all the countries where Jews were living their faith and religion exercised a powerful attraction on their pagan neighbours, and yet these admirers remained for the most part outsiders, because if they became proselytes they must needs come within the Jewish nation and forsake their own.

Our Lord's ministry was entirely or almost entirely to Jews: 'I am not sent but unto the lost sheep of the house of Israel' (Matt. 15. 24). Yet within a few years of His resurrection Gentiles were being freely admitted within the Church. St. Luke records three independent initiatives in this direction, those of Philip (Acts 8. 26–40), of Peter (Acts 10), and of unnamed Christians at Antioch (Acts 11. 20). The Ethiopian is convinced by Philip of the fulfilment in Jesus of Isa. 53. Cornelius and his friends accept the Gospel, and they receive the gift of the Holy Ghost; Peter meanwhile has had his scruples about eating with Gentiles taken away by a vision which confirmed the Master's own teaching which he had heard long before (Mark 7. 15). When on Peter's return to Jerusalem the Jewish Christians there questioned his action, doubting whether these Gentiles should not have become Jews first, before being accepted as Christians, Peter told his story: the Messianic Gift of the Spirit had been given to the Gentiles, as to themselves at Pentecost; it was the hand of the LORD, and there was no more to be said.

But for years discussions and heart-searching went on: it became the first great controversy in the Church, in which St. Paul played a leading part, insisting that the Gospel was for all nations. In his Epistle to the Galatians he insists that the gift of the Holy Spirit is the sign that the Messianic Age has begun, and the share of the Gentiles in this gift proves that they are called to be members of God's Israel. Those who insist that all Gentile converts must be circumcised and become Jews first, are acting as if the Messiah had not come, and the Holy Spirit had not been given.

Yet on the other side there was something to be said. The best Jewish Christians were rightly anxious lest the Church should be flooded with converts who did not know the Old Testament, and the way of living in which Jews were brought up: would there not soon appear in the Church a pagan way of thinking and a pagan laxity of morals? There was reason for both these fears: some at Corinth are found denying the resurrection of the body (1 Cor. 15. 12), others falling into scandalous sins and abuses of Christian freedom (1 Cor. 5. 1; 8. 10). The Gentile had very much to learn from the Jew.

St. Paul saw both sides. His life-work, in one aspect, was

a great battle for the unity of the Church, as embracing Jews
and Gentiles. The truth which he had to proclaim was
two-sided. The one side was that the period of Ezra's
Judaism was now over: the promises made by the prophets
of the Exile were being fulfilled. The legal righteousness of
the Pharisees belonged now to the past—that is, the notion
that the way to please God was to keep the letter of the
Law: that belonged to the period of Judaism, to the period
before the Messiah had come. Now He had come, and
He had been crucified: by His death the law-keeping
Pharisee and the licentious pagan were declared to be equally
sinners and equally objects of God's mercy: 'God hath
shut up all unto disobedience, that he might have mercy
upon all' (Rom. 11. 32). To all alike salvation comes by
Grace, that is, by God's free gift.

The other side was that the Law was God's Law, 'holy
and righteous and good'. The evil that appeared under
the Law, and that had brought Christ to the cross, and that
had been exhibited with full clearness in Paul's own life
when he had been a Pharisee, was not the fault of the Law,
but of the self-centredness of the self, that had made law-
keeping a matter of pride. The Law was good, and the
Gentiles needed it; they needed the whole Old Testament,
Law as well as Prophets. And none knew better than Paul
how they needed rules for the sake of discipline; they too
must learn the lessons that the Jew had learnt in the synagogue. He gave rules to his Corinthians and expected them
to be kept.

It was not altogether easy for them. The Law was God's
Law; yet as Law it had passed away; Christians were not
to be circumcised nor to offer animal sacrifices, for the
Christ had come. Yet the principles of the Law remained,
for in Him the Law was not destroyed but fulfilled. How,

then, in detail, were the Christians from among the Gentiles to use the Old Testament ? This is the question with which we were posed at the beginning of this book. In the light of what has been said, we will try in a last chapter to draw together the main principles of the answer.

On the earliest Christian preaching (cf. p. 144) :

    C. H. Dodd, *The Apostolic Preaching and its Developments.* Hodder & Stoughton, 1935.

On the fulfilment of the Old Testament in Christ :

    E. C. Hoskyns and F. N. Davey, *The Riddle of the New Testament.* Faber, 1931.

    R. C. P. Hanson and C. Harvey, *The Loom of God.* A.P.C.K., Dublin, 1945.

    R. V. G. Tasker, *The Old Testament in the New Testament.* S.C.M., 1946. (Macmillan.)

On the fulfilment of sacrifice (cf. pp. 165–7) :

    A. G. Hebert, *The Throne of David.* Faber, 1941. (pp. 111–22 and Ch. VIII.) (Morehouse.)

CHAPTER XII

' *To Him bear all the prophets witness* '

THE CHRISTIAN USE OF THE OLD TESTAMENT

How, then, do Christians use the Old Testament?

First let us notice this. No Christian thinks that he is bound to do all the things which it commands; even the fundamentalist, who holds that the Bible contains the literal commandments of God, flatly disobeys the plain directions of the Bible that he must circumcise his male children, may on no account eat pork or bacon, may do no work on Saturday, and must get rid of every bit of leaven out of his house before Easter. Yet these four things (chosen at random) are all plainly laid down in the Bible: see Gen. 17. 10; Lev. 11. 7; Exod. 20. 10; 12. 15. We disregard these commands because in the tradition of the Christian Church which we have inherited these things are not done, and the Church's tradition is supported by the plain teaching of our Lord and His Apostles in the New Testament.

In each case, however, the principle holds that He ' came not to destroy but to fulfil ' the Law and the Prophets (Matt. 5. 17). It is not that He rejected the Law and upheld the Prophets, nor that He rejected the ceremonial Law and upheld the moral Law: it is that He came to ' fulfil ' both, and, as we have seen, transform them in fulfilling them. Consequently, in each of these four points, while the commandment is rejected, there is a positive principle involved in it which holds good.

171   M

We do not circumcise the children. St. Paul explains to the Galatians that the rite of circumcision belongs to the pre-Christian dispensation, and if the Galatians insist on going back to circumcision, they will be acting as if Christ had not come, as if the Promises had not been fulfilled, and the Holy Ghost had not been given (Gal. 5. 2–6; 6. 11–18). For Christians there is baptism, which is the sacrament of their new birth into Christian sonship (Gal. 3. 26–8). Yet, as he points out elsewhere, circumcision had a spiritual meaning, which had found clear expression in the Old Testament : ' circumcise therefore the foreskin of your heart, and be no more stiff-necked ' (Deut. 10. 16) ; ' the LORD thy God will circumcise thy heart and the heart of thy seed, to love the LORD thy God with all thy heart and with all thy soul, that thou mayest live ' (Deut. 30. 6). St. Paul picks this point up in Rom. 2. 27–9 and Col. 2. 11 ; it is further drawn out in the Epistle and the proper Lessons for the feast of our Lord's Circumcision on 1 January, and in the Collect : ' Grant us the true circumcision of the Spirit, that our hearts and all our members being mortified from all worldly and carnal lusts, we may in all things obey Thy blessed will.'

We are quite happy in eating pork and bacon, because the rules given in Lev. 11 about the foods which were prohibited as being ' unclean ' were abrogated by our LORD : ' There is nothing from without a man that going into him can defile him : but the things which proceed out of a man are those that defile the man ' (Mark 7. 15). This is explained further in the following verses : we become unclean only by speaking unclean words and thinking unclean thoughts (Mark 7. 18–23). But long before this, prophets and psalmists had spoken of sin as the real ' defilement ' : ' Wash you, make you clean, put away the evil of your doings from before mine eyes' (Isa. 1. 16) : 'Wash me thoroughly from my wickedness, and cleanse me from my sin' (Ps. 51. 2). According to the Law, there was a ceremonial 'uncleanness' which could be incurred by eating 'unclean' foods, touching a leper, touching a dead body, and in other ways ; and this ritual uncleanness disqualified an Israelite from approaching the Sanctuary, and cut him off from fellowship with the community. In God's education of Israel, this was the means by which the people learnt, first, that there can be acts which cut them off from God and from their fellow-men, and then, that this is what Sin does.

We do not keep the Sabbath-law, because the Sabbath of the Old Law is now seen to have been an ordinance with a symbolical meaning, looking forward to the Rest on which the People of God would enter in the Future Age. 'There remaineth therefore a Sabbath-rest for the people of God' (Heb. 4. 9) : God, who rested on the Seventh Day after the work of creation, calls man to enter into this Rest. So when our Lord came, He spoke of Himself as 'Lord of the Sabbath' (Mark 2. 28), and He treated the Sabbath as the day on which it was especially appropriate to do His Messianic works of healing : see Luke 13. 10–16. The Fathers speak of our whole Christian life as a sharing in our Lord's Sabbath ; and a favourite hymn speaks of 'Heaven' in these terms :

> There dawns no Sabbath, no Sabbath is o'er,
> Those Sabbath-keepers have one and no more,
> One and unending is that triumph-song
> Which to the angels and us shall belong.

'Peace I leave with you : My peace I give unto you' (John 14. 27) ; that peace is the fulfilment of the Sabbath. There is further the principle of one day's rest in seven : but the day which is thus kept as holy to the LORD has from

the very beginning been 'the first day of the week', the
day of the Lord's resurrection: thus we find the Christians
at Troas in St. Paul's time meeting 'on the first day of the
week' to 'break bread', i.e. to celebrate the Holy Eucharist
(Acts 20. 7).

We disregard the rule about leaven, in the same way.
St. Paul says 'Purge out the old leaven, that ye may be a
new lump, even as ye are unleavened. For our Passover
also has been sacrificed, even Christ: wherefore let us keep
the Feast, not with the old leaven, neither with the leaven of
malice and wickedness, but with the unleavened bread of
sincerity and truth' (1 Cor. 5. 7–8). The 'new lump'
(*phurāma*) of which St. Paul speaks is an allusion to Exod. 12.
34, where the Israelites, escaping out of Egypt, take their
baking-materials with them; but it has been suggested that
St. Paul is thinking also of Num. 15. 18–20, where it is said
that, when they enter the Promised Land, they must 'offer
up a cake' of the first bread which they eat there, as a heave-
offering to the LORD. In becoming Christians, they have
escaped out of Egypt, and entered the Promised Land: the
'cake' which they must offer is their own lives, offered up
to the LORD for His service. For as when Israel came out
of Egypt they ate the Passover Lamb in the sacrifice that
they offered then, so in the Second Exodus Christ is the
Passover sacrifice; and the crisp, hard unleavened bread
of the old rite is now represented by the crispness of Christian
sincerity and truth.

The thoughts which are set before us by the New Testament in these four instances are typical of the use which is
made of the Old Testament in the New. In each case,
what we are shown is a *picture*, taken from the Old Testament,
and used to illuminate the saving work of Christ and the
life of Christians in the Church.

PICTURE-LANGUAGE

The Old Testament speaks throughout in the language of pictures. Its marvellous stories draw pictures for us, which remain in our minds : the Ark riding in the waters of the Flood, Abraham sacrificing Isaac, Jacob's dream at Bethel, Joseph in Egypt, the Crossing of the Red Sea ; David slaying Goliath, David the king, Elijah on Mount Carmel— these and many more stories. There is the glory of the sanctuary, the Presence on the sacred Ark, the smoke of the burnt-offering ascending as a sweet savour to the LORD. There are the visions of the glory of the LORD seen by Isaiah, of the cherub-chariot in Ezekiel, of the Son of Man in Daniel chapter 7, of the Servant of the LORD in Second Isaiah.

A wealth of imagery is drawn from the common things of universal experience : light and darkness, food, drink, shelter, raiment. It is worth considering how the imagery of Light is used. There was the Light in the beginning of the creation, when God said ' let there be light' (Gen. 1. 2) ; the fire that gleamed in the Pillar of Cloud : the light and fire in the cherub-chariot (Ezek. 1. 13, 14, 27). So ' the LORD is my light and my salvation : whom then shall I fear ?' (Ps. 27. 1). Looking forward to the Messianic days, the prophet says ' The people that sat in darkness have seen a great light' (Isa. 9. 2) and ' Arise, shine, for thy light is come' (Isa. 60. 1). When the Saviour comes, there is the Star of Matt. 2, and the text from Isa. 9. 2 is quoted for Him as He begins His ministry, in Matt. 4. 16. In His Transfiguration His face shines as the sun (Matt. 17. 2). For He is ' the Light of the World ', so that he who follows Him shall not walk in darkness but shall have the light of life (John 8. 12). But the coming of the Light is terrible to men who live in the darkness, and shrink from coming to the Light lest their works should be reproved and shown to be evil (John 3. 19); yet this coming to the Light is the acceptance of salvation; 'while ye have the Light, believe in the Light, that ye may become sons of light' (John 12. 36). To the darkness belong deeds such as the work of the thief, the adulterer, the drunkard, and the night is the time of sleep (Rom. 12. 11–14; 1 Thess. 5. 4–8): but for the Christians 'the night is far spent and the day is at hand', and they are sons of light and sons of the day (ibid.). The Heavenly City has no need of the sun or of the moon to shine upon it, for the glory of God illuminates it and the Lamb is the light thereof (Rev. 21. 23).

Here we see the imagery of Light used to describe the work of God in the whole order of creation and of redemption; and it dwells in the imagination as exact theological definitions cannot do. The dogma of the Incarnation is principally set forth in this way. The Bible does not speak of Our Lord as the Second Person of the Trinity, having two natures in one Person : it shows Him to us as the Son of Man, the Servant of the Lord, *Immanuel* or God-with-us, the Effulgence of the Father's Glory, the Word of the Father, the King, the High-Priest, the Lamb offered in sacrifice, the Shepherd of the Flock.

It is through such picture-language that the truths of the Faith impress themselves upon the mind; the exposition of this picture-language is therefore a primary duty of the Christian pastor. It can make a vast difference to the sermons that are preached, if the preacher can equip himself not merely for teaching dogma in abstract theological language, but for presenting it and letting it make its appeal through that same pictorial language in which the Bible gives it—drawing out the imagery of the Wedding-feast to which all are invited by the King, that they may sup with Him;

or what the Bible means by the Name of God, and the Name of Jesus, and each person's Christian name; or the offering of prayer as incense, as in Rev. 8. 3–5; or such words of His own lips as ' Behold, I stand at the door and knock ', or ' Be of good cheer; it is I; be not afraid.' Such pictorial imagery speaks to us directly, as no theological formula can ever do.

Yet there is danger in the use of imagery. The image of the Messianic King can be applied to a Hitler; that of the Chosen People was used to support the Nazi creed. Imagery appeals to the imagination; and the use of it, uncontrolled by right reason, can lead to dangerous fanaticisms, making a claim to inspiration. But not all ' inspiration ' is true inspiration. In the Old Testament there are ' false prophets ' as well as the true prophets of God; in the New Testament St. John says, ' Beloved, believe not every spirit, but prove the spirits, whether they are of God, because many false prophets are gone out into the world ' (1 John 4. 1), and his criterion is whether the prophets acknowledge the true manhood of Jesus the Son of God. St. John asserts the need for a control of ' inspiration ' by sound theology.

The definitions of orthodox theology are necessary to relate our religious language with our general knowledge about the world and man, and with what we call common sense. The great dogmatic definitions which were framed by the Church of the fourth and fifth centuries, about the Incarnation and the Holy Trinity, related the Christian Faith to philosophical thought in such a way as to exclude pagan and sub-Christian notions of God, and protect the Biblical faith of the Church from corruption. The creeds, which took shape in the first place as the confession of faith made by a Christian at his baptism, remain the essential safeguard of the faith of the Scriptures.

Behind the orthodox theology lies the revelation of God in history ; and though the Bible does not give us a systematic theology, its picture-language is controlled at every point by the historical revelation of the LORD God to old Israel and in Christ. It is for this reason that in this book we have been at pains to set out the framework of the Biblical history, in order to show the actual development of the Faith in the course of the history, as a story of God's dealing with Israel His People, which finds its crown and fulfilment in the person of Christ and His saving work. It is necessary for the Christian to have a clear idea of the course of the Biblical history, in order that he may read the books aright. As the theologians insist, the primary meaning of Scripture is its literal meaning, that is to say, the meaning which the writers intended to convey by the words which they wrote ; and we have seen how this literal and true meaning of the Old Testament leads up to Christ, and the history finds its actual fulfilment in Jesus.

THE INTERPRETATION OF THE BIBLE

The line of interpretation of the Bible which has been followed in this book starts from seeking to find out and understand the plain and literal meaning of each part of it, that is, the meaning which each writer intended to convey by the words which he used ; he meant what he said, and we must try to interpret his meaning correctly and truly. It is important to do this, both for the sake of literary honesty, and because the Bible history is a history of real events, of the lives of real men and women. It is through such a history that God has accomplished His saving work for Israel and for mankind.

But because the Bible is the story of a Purpose of God worked out in history, and fulfilled in Jesus Christ, our

Lord and His Apostles in the New Testament interpret His saving work in the light of the Messianic prophecies. Those prophecies had traced a series of patterns and correspondences between the first redemption in the time of Moses and the future Messianic redemption; and the New Testament shows how these patterns have been worked out in the story of Jesus Christ. We have seen how they say that ' Christ our Passover is sacrificed for us '; His death and resurrection are a second Exodus, leading to the establishment of a New Covenant. This means that when the Apostles read the stories of the Exodus and the Covenant at Horeb, or used a psalm such as ' When Israel came out of Egypt ' (Ps. 114), they saw these as types of our Lord's redemptive work; and the Church does the same, in appointing these psalms and lessons to be read at Easter and Pentecost.

The plain and literal meaning of the New Testament writers, when they are seeking to interpret the meaning of our Lord's saving work, is that they do this by use of the pictorial imagery of the Old Testament. Similarly, the plain and literal meaning of Jeremiah, as he looks forward to the future Messianic Deliverance, is that he sees this taking place according to the pattern of the Exodus and the Covenant under Moses; and it follows that when Jeremiah read (as he did) those of the narratives preserved in our Book of Exodus which were available to him, he saw those stories not only as records of past history, but also as ' types ' of the future Deliverance. In other words, the stories had for him a ' spiritual ' or ' mystical ' meaning.

Here we are at a point about which much discussion is going on. From the time of the Fathers of the early church, the ' allegorical ' method of interpreting the Bible has been much used, and much misused. Believing that the Bible was the word of God, but not being able to find any edifying meaning in large parts of it, as for instance in the Old Testament stories, men looked for a 'spiritual' meaning hidden beneath the natural meaning, and took the story as an allegory. A famous instance is that of Rahab hanging a scarlet thread from her window in the wall of Jericho, that when the city is destroyed she and her family may be saved (Josh. 2. 18–21 ; 6. 22–5) ; this was to be taken to mean that the king of Jericho is the Devil, the city is the world falling under God's judgement, and the red thread is the blood of Christ whereby we are saved.

It is not hard to criticize this method of interpretation, first, because it appears to be completely arbitrary ; as someone has said, according to it ' anything can mean anything '. Then again, the interpretation has nothing to do with the original meaning intended by the writer. Again, the story is not being treated seriously as history, for it would make an equally good allegory if it were a fable ; and indeed, according to this way of interpretation, the Bible would cease to be a history, and would become a book of oracles for ingenious people to decipher. Yet again, when we have learnt that the red thread means the blood of Christ, no fresh light whatever has been thrown on the meaning of our Lord's redemptive death. Perhaps, in this instance, there is just one valid point in the interpretation : namely that, as our Lord in Luke 17. 26–30 takes the Flood and the Destruction of Sodom as types or pictures of the Last Judgement, it could be right to do the same with Jericho, which would thus rank with the City of Destruction in the *Pilgrim's Progress*, as a type of the world under God's judgement.

Is it possible to find some valid criterion by which to distinguish right and wrong sorts of 'spiritual interpretation' ? That is the question ; and it does seem that the line which has been followed in this book provides at least the beginnings of the right answer.

The Messianic prophecies of the Old Testament and their fulfilment in Christ have here been taken as the chief line of connexion between the Old Testament and the New ; for it is not only that these prophecies were applied by the Apostles to our Lord's life, but also that He did His work in the light of them. At the Last Supper He believed that He was establishing the New Covenant. Here we are assuredly on firm ground, indeed on the broad high-road of sound Biblical interpretation. The Old Testament history is treated as history, the prophecies are seen in their place in the historical development, and the effort is made to interpret the New Testament teaching in its proper meaning. The imagery used by our Lord and the Apostles is quite unlike the instance just given of Rahab's scarlet thread ; for a clear light is shed on the meaning of our Lord's passion when, for instance, He is declared to be ' our Passover, sacrificed for us ', or to be the ' Servant of the LORD '.

Much more would need to be said in order to give a satisfactory theological account of the New Testament use of imagery ; such an account would be over-technical for this book. We will then content ourselves with some observations on two important themes, the meaning of the Passion, and the Christian use of the Psalms.

THE WAY OF THE HOLY CROSS

Our Lord Himself said several times (e.g. Mark 9. 12–13) that it was prophesied that the Christ should suffer ; and this was the main teaching which He gave to the two disciples on the way to Emmaus :

And he said unto them, ' O foolish men, and slow of heart to believe in all that the prophets have spoken. Behoved it not the Christ to suffer these things, and to enter into his glory?' And beginning from Moses and from all the prophets, he expounded to them in all the scriptures the things concerning himself. (Luke 24. 25–7; cf. 44–7.)

In Luke 22. 37 He quoted from Isa. 53 the words 'He was numbered with the transgressors'; and at the Last Supper, in the eucharistic words, He interpreted His death as sacrificial. (Mark 14. 22–4; 1 Cor. 11. 23–5.)

But He pointed not only to what the prophets said about salvation through suffering, but also to what they themselves suffered. Thus in His parable of the Wicked Husbandmen (Mark 12. 1–10) the Vineyard is Israel, and the Servants whom the Lord sends to demand from the husbandmen the fruits of the vineyard are the Prophets; they are rejected and maltreated, and some of them are killed. Last of all, He sends His only-beloved Son, and He is killed likewise. The same teaching is given in Matt. 23. 34–6: 'Behold, I send unto you prophets and wise men and scribes: some of them ye shall kill and crucify' and scourge and persecute, that on you may come all the righteous blood shed on the earth from the first murder in Genesis, that of Abel, to the last murder in the Book of Chronicles, that of Zechariah: 'verily I say unto you, all these things shall come upon this generation'. For the coming of the Messiah is a dramatic climax in which the whole previous history is gathered up.

Our Lord knew that the road along which He must go was 'the royal road of the Holy Cross'. The prophets had trodden that road before Him; His own disciples must tread it after Him, for 'If any man will come after Me let him deny himself and take up his cross' (Mark 8. 34); for whoever was determined to achieve his own salvation in his own way would lose everything, but whoever was prepared to throw away his life for the Master's sake and the Gospel's sake would find that it had all been kept safe for him (paraphrase of 8. 35). So in the Epistles Christians are told to be content to suffer, if suffering comes on them, 'because Christ suffered for us, leaving us an example that ye should follow His steps' (see 1 Pet. 2. 21–5 ; cf. 4. 12–13). The panegyric in Heb. 11. 33–8 on the heroes of the Faith (quoted on p. 134 above), itself largely taken from the memories of the Maccabean persecution, was also a description in advance of the sufferings which the Christian Church was to endure for 250 years in the persecutions which were just beginning when that chapter was written.

Thus we see the cross of our Lord standing at the central point of the world's history : and both before and after it a long series of similar sufferings and martyrdoms, endured in faith and hope. But His cross stands at the centre ; and their sufferings become victorious because the Son of God Himself has entered the battle and won through His sufferings the central and decisive victory. The Seer in the Book of the Revelation weeps because the Book (of the prophecies which interpret history) is sealed and cannot be opened ; then it is said to him : 'Weep not : behold, the Lion which is of the tribe of Judah, the Root of David, hath overcome, to open the book and the seven seals thereof' (Rev. 5. 1–5). And He who is the Lion is also the Lamb of sacrifice, seen not lying dead but living through death (verse 6).

CHRIST IN THE PSALMS

We have, then, through the Old Testament, a series of partial lights, examples of righteousness, witnesses to truth, servants of the LORD found faithful unto death : and we have in Christ the Light of the World, the Righteousness of God manifested in His true humanity, the King who is *the*

Witness to the truth (John 18. 37), *the* Servant of the LORD. In Him they are vindicated. In Him, whatever is imperfect in them is done away, and whatever is true shines out in its fullness.

Here is the principle which underlies the Church's recitation of the Psalms. The Jews collected the Psalms into a psalter, and recited them in Temple and synagogue, as the prayer of the believing and worshipping community. The Christians took over this practice : but when they used the old psalms, it was as the utterance of Christian prayer made in common in the Name of Christ, in union with His heavenly intercession as the High-priest and the Head of the Body. Some psalms would be seen at once to have an obvious reference to Him, such as Ps. 22, the psalm of His passion, or Ps. 72, the psalm of His universal Kingdom. But all the psalms were seen to be His. In them many voices are heard, praising God and giving Him thanks, trusting Him wholly, accepting His providential care, confessing sin both corporate and personal, calling to Him out of the darkness of perplexity and of that which, without this calling on Him, would be despair, praying for deliverance from sickness and death, from all evil, and from cruel enemies, giving thanks on behalf of the Israel of God and remembering God's mighty works : for the psalms cover the whole range of human need.

So the meaning of the Psalms, thus used as the Church's common praise and prayer, is that the Son of God has taken to Himself our human nature. In the Incarnation He came to claim fellowship with men, ' not to be ministered unto, but to minister ' and to bear men's burdens in fullness of sympathy. Thus the Psalms become His psalms.

This can be, even though they are the work of imperfect men. Thus for instance Ps. 54, ' Save me, O God, for

Thy Name's sake', is a supplication to God made by one who is beset by enemies, and prays for their destruction : he is perplexed, with his back to the wall, contending for the victory of God's cause, and sure that God's cause will at last prevail. If this psalm were used by our Lord, it would be a prayer that the suffering which lay before Him in the course of His mission might lead to His resurrection-victory. It was so used by Him, no doubt, in the days of His flesh : and it bears this meaning for us as we use it in the Church.

As our Lord was able to accept Israel, with all its faults, as the People of God, and identify Himself with it, that the Purpose of God for which He had chosen it to be His people might be at last fulfilled, so that there might be salvation for mankind, even though the cost were His sufferings and death on the Cross, so He could accept the Psalms. As He went to His agony in the Garden of Gethsemane, it seems that Ps. 42 was on His lips ; for when the words ' *My soul* is *exceeding sorrowful* even unto death ' (Mark 14. 34) are read in St. Mark's Greek, the words in italics are the same as the words ' Why art thou so *vexed*, O *my soul* ' in the Greek version of Ps. 42. 5. On the cross He used the words of Ps. 22. 1 ' My God, my God, why hast Thou forsaken me ? ' (Mark 15. 34). The prophet had said that the victory of God would be won by the faithful Remnant. In His Passion, the faithful Remnant was represented by Himself alone, contending for the victory of God's cause, the deliverance of men from the powers of darkness, and the coming of God's Kingdom ; and there the victory was won which became manifest in His Resurrection. ' Be of good cheer : I have overcome the world ' (John 16. 33).

THE BIBLE AND THE CHURCH

Thus the Bible is the book of the Church, which is the

Israel of God. Both under the Old Covenant and the New it presupposes a visible society, called into existence by God for the accomplishment of His saving purpose for mankind. This visible society rests on the acts of God in history, in the first redemption when He called Israel out of Egypt and made His Covenant with it, and in the second redemption when He came in person to fight His own battle and effect man's deliverance from the last Enemy of man. This visible society is always imperfect: in the Bible we see a continuous conflict going on within Israel itself between faith and unbelief, between faithfulness and disloyalty, and we see the same conflict continuing in the Church and in our own hearts, where the Spirit of God is perpetually at war with the lustfulness and selfishness of man. Yet in spite of all its imperfections and sins, Israel remained the People of God and the Church is still His Church. In our times the visible society has become divided, and has become split up into 'denominations': nine centuries ago there came the breach between Eastern and Western Christendom, and four centuries ago a further series of divisions in Western Christendom which continue to this day. Yet the denominations agree in this, that they all accept and use the Bible.

They act as denominations when they live their separate lives, estranged from one another. But when they go back to their Bible, they find there not the many denominations, but the one Church of God; one with a unity which cannot be broken, since it is constituted by the Purpose of God for man's salvation and by the Word of God Who became incarnate and took to Himself the Church as His Body, as His Bride, as His Temple, as His Flock.

In our day there has arisen a great longing for the reunion of divided Christendom. The peril and the great temptation of Christians to-day is to interpret this reunion of Christendom as an amalgamation of denominations for the sake of greater efficiency in organization, and greater effectiveness in work. Such amalgamation of denominations can never produce the unity of the Church of God. There can be no true unity except in a return into the unity which God has made, in a spirit of faith and of penitence.

Perhaps the greatest assurance that we have that the unity of the Church really is on the way is the fact that in our day a Biblical Theology has arisen, which draws together the men of the different denominations in the common study of the Bible as the Book of the Israel of God and of His Purpose for mankind : for it is impossible to study the Bible as Holy Scripture without coming to see that it presupposes the one Church of God, and learning from it to understand the meaning of our churchmanship. Those who thus study the Bible together cannot fail at last (by God's mercy) to repent of their denominationalism, and come to agree in the truth of His holy word, and thereby be led into a true unity resting on a common faith, and live in unity and godly love.

Four centuries ago we had the schisms of the Reformation period ; nine centuries ago the breach between the East and the West ; nineteen centuries ago the breach between the Christians and the Jews. If Catholic and Protestant Christians, and Western and Eastern Orthodox Christians, know that in spite of the schisms they have a common ancestry in the undivided Church, Christians and Jews know that they too have a common ancestry in the Church of God under the Old Covenant. And when the Jews see that the Christians are again taking the Old Testament seriously, and delighting to think of ourselves as the Israel of God, we can hope that they will not be willing to be left out of this study, and that a new sort of contact between

Christians and Jews will spring up, and the estrangement which has existed for nineteen centuries will pass away. In the Old Testament we and they have a common ancestry. The unity of the Church of God cannot be complete without them.

On the law of uncleanness, and of the Sabbath :

    A. G. Hebert, *The Throne of David.* Faber, 1941. (pp. 98–103 and Ch. VI.)   (Morehouse.)

On imagery :

    A. M. Farrer, *The Glass of Vision* (Bampton Lectures).   Dacre Press, 1948.   Esp. Lectures VI and VII.

On mystical interpretation :

    A. G. Hebert, *The Authority of the Old Testament.* Faber, 1947.   Ch. IX.

On the Bible and the Church :

    A. M. Ramsey, *The Gospel and the Catholic Church.* Longmans, 1936.

AN INDEX OF NAMES AND SUBJECTS

Abimelech, 43
Abraham, 4, 5, 7, 38–44
Acts, Book of the, 144
Actual Sin, 31–2
Adam and Eve, 2, 8, 23–8, 31
Advent, the Second, 162
Ahab, king, 35
Ahaz, king, 70
Allegorical interpretation, 179–80
Amos, 48, 63–6, 99, 109
Antiochus Epiphanes, 125, 132–7
Apostolic preaching, the, 144
Ark of the Covenant, the, 105–6,
    163
Assyria, 69–72, 80

Baals, 16, 36–7, 66–7, 76, 78
Baptism, 144, 172
Batho, D., 124
Belshazzar, 136
Bevan, E., 140
Bible, beginnings of the, 77, 86–9,
    115
Bridegroom and Bride, 55, 67–8
Burning Fiery Furnace, 135

Caesar, tribute to, 153
Canaanite religion, 16, 36, 63,
    66–7, 70, 75
Christ the King, 146–54
Chronicles, Books of, 112, 125–7
Church, the, 3–4, 68, 88, 111, 153,
    160–2, 167–70, 174, 177,
    183–4, 185–8
Circumcision, 171–2
Clarendon Bible, the, 62, 79, 124
Cleansing of the Temple, 151
Coggin, F. E., 22, 33
Collingwood, R. G., 62

Converted nation, 78, 104
Covenant, 54–5, 74, 81, 89–90,
    102–4, 114–16, 154–8, 181
Creation, the, 12–22, 89, 129–32,
    160–1
Cross, the, 151, 181–3
Curse attached to crucifixion, the,
    151

Daniel, 134–7, 139
Davey, F. N., 170
David, 57, 59, 60, 117, 126, 158
Day of the Lord, the, 65, 99, 100,
    107–8, 113, 139, 143, 159
Deism, 17
Demant, V. A., 22
Democracy, 19
Denominations, 4, 186–7
Deuteronomy, 48, 52–4, 74–9, 85,
    115, 122
Dodd, C. H., 11, 170
Driver, S. R., 22

Ecclesiasticus, 130
Elliott-Binns, T. H., 62
Elmslie, W. A. L., 79
Ephesians, Epistle to the, 6–7, 111
Esau, 44
Evans, C. F., 11
Exile, the, 82, 86–9, 112–14
Exodus, the, 4, 50–4, 98, 101–2,
    146, 153, 174
Ezekiel, 62, 82–4, 97–8, 104,
    106–7, 140
Ezra, 86, 112–16, 119–20, 125,
    138, 167

Faith of Abraham, 39–41
Fall of Man, 23, 25–9

189

AN INDEX OF NAMES AND SUBJECTS

False gods to-day, 17
Farrer, A. M., 188
Father, 47–8
Flood, story of the, 73–4, 180
Freedom, 149
Fulfilment, meaning of, 145, 146, 164–6, 181
Fundamentalism, 1, 15, 171
Future Life, the, 136

Galatians, Epistle to the, 168
Gentiles, 109–11, 121–4, 167–70
Gideon, 37, 56
Glory of the LORD, 106, 163–4
Goudge, H. L., 11
Graeco-Roman religion, 36
Greek influence on Israel, 127–37

Hagar, 39, 42–3
Haggai, 113
Hananiah, 82
Hanson, R. C. P., and Harvey, C., 170
Hebert, A. G., 11, 22, 96, 111, 170, 188
Hebrews, Epistle to the, 20–1, 39, 40–1, 134, 136, 145, 166–7
Hezekiah, king, 100
Hinduism, 36
History, 5–6, 48–9, 56–9, 116–18, 125–6, 178
Hosea, 55, 66–8
Hoskyns, E. C., 170
Hypocrite, 149

Imagery, 175–8
Incarnation, the, 20–1, 176
Isaac, 40, 41, 44
Isaiah, 64–5, 69–74, 99–100, 109, 146
Isaiah, Second, 13–14, 86, 89, 90–6, 102, 107–8, 109–10, 141
Ishmael, 42–3

Jacob, 44–5
Jehovah, 11
Jeremiah, 65–6, 77–8, 82, 85, 101–2, 140, 154, 179
Jews, the, 187–8
Job, 127, 130
Joel, 104
John, St., 111, 132, 152, 161, 164
Jonah, 121–2
Joseph, 45–6
Joshua, 56
Josiah, king, 74–6
Judaism, post-exilic, 115–40
Judas Maccabeus, 133
Judges, the, 37
Justification through Faith, 158

Kingdom of God, 141, 148–54
Knowledge of good and evil, 27

Lamb of God, 31, 41
Law, 19
Law, the Mosaic, 29, 55, 117, 130, 137–40, 155–6, 169, 171–4
Leaven, 171, 174
Lewis, C. S., 33
Light, imagery of, 175–6
Literal meaning of Scripture, 178–9
Lofthouse, W. F., 124
Lot, 39
Lowther Clarke, W. K., 11

Maccabees, Books of the, 133
Malachi, 113, 138, 141
Man in God's image, 18–20, 89
Manoah, 59
Manson, T. W., 11
Maurice, F. D., 28, 46
Messiah, the, 107, 146
Messianic prophecies, 97–111, 144–5, 179
Miracles, 110, 142
Missionaries, 111

Monotheism, 61
Moses, 50–4, 116–18

Nationalism, 17, 140
Nebuchadnezzar, 82, 134–6
Nehemiah, 112–16, 125, 167
New Creation, the, 21–2
Nicodemus, 162
Noah, Covenant with, 89–90
North, C., 62

Oesterley, W. O. E., and Robinson, T. H., 124
Original Sin, 31–3

Paul, St., 123, 155, 168–9
Pentecost, 143–4
Persecution, 133–7
Peter, St., 144, 145, 157, 167–8
Pharisees, the, 32, 137–40, 149, 155–6
Phillips, G. E., 46
Phythian-Adams, W. J., 51, 62
Picture-language, 175–8
Plagues of Egypt, 51
Presence, the, 105–7, 118–19, 163–7
Priestly document, the, 34, 89, 116–19
Proverbs, Book of, 128–30
Psalms, *passim and* 183–6
Psalm 42, 185
Psalm 119, 138
Purpose of God, 5–6, 39–40, 46, 58, 74, 78, 81, 86, 104, 108–9, 150, 178–9

Rahab, 180–1
Ramsey, A. M., 188
Reality of God, 48, 61
Remnant, doctrine of the, 72–4, 99, 185
Resurrection of Christ, 41, 157

Revelation, Book of the, 21, 33, 71–2, 165, 183
Richardson, A., 11
Righteousness, 155–6
Rowley, H. H., 62, 124
Ruth, 122

Sabbath, 15, 114, 133, 139, 171–4
Sacrifice, fulfilment of, 165–7
Sacrifice of Isaac, 40–1
Samaritans, 125–6
Samuel, 37, 56, 64
Sarah, 39, 43
Saul, 37, 56, 60
Savagery, 60
Schools of the prophets, 38, 46
Sciences, 131
Scribes, 139, 142
Sennacherib, 35, 70–1
Septuagint, 127
Serpent, the, 25–6
Servant of the LORD, 90–6
Shakespeare, 2–3
Shepherd, 163
Sin, 26–33
Smith, G. A., 79, 96
Sodom, 39, 180
Solomon, king, 27, 117
Son of Man, 136–7, 143, 148
Spirit, the Holy, 103–5, 154, 158–63, 168
Suffering, meaning of, 90, 181–3
Synagogue, 87–9, 123, 138

Tabernacle, 105, 116–19, 164–5
Tasker, R. V. G., 170
Temple, 75, 80, 106, 113, 118, 125, 143, 151, 164–5
Theology, 177–8
Transgression, 30
Trinity, doctrine of the, 20

Unclean foods, 133, 171–3
Unity of the Church, 169, 186–8

Valley of Dry Bones, the, 84

Wand, Bp., 11
Wisdom, 128–32
Wisdom, Book of, 130–2
Woman who was a sinner, the, 149–50

Word of God, the, 132
Writing on the Wall, 136

Zealots, 140
Zechariah, 113
Zerubbabel, 113